Surrendering to, Believing in, Living for, and Proclaiming Your True Identity!

TRANSFORMATION

William Lee Ioerger

WESTBOW°
PRESS
A DIVISION OF THOMAS NELSON
& ZONDERVAN

WestBow Press books may be ordered through booksellers or by contacting:

WestBow Press
A Division of Thomas Nelson & Zondervan
1663 Liberty Drive
Bloomington, IN 47403
www.westbowpress.com
1 (866) 928-1240

ISBN: 978-1-4908-8469-1 (sc)
ISBN: 978-1-4908-8470-7 (hc)
ISBN: 978-1-4908-8468-4 (e)

Library of Congress Control Number: 2015909631

Print information available on the last page.

WestBow Press rev. date: 06/22/2015

Contents

PROCLAIM

He who overcomes, I will make him a pillar in the temple of My God, and he shall go out no more.

—Revelation 3:12

Acknowledgments

God has blessed my wife, Teresa, and me with many wonderful new friends during our personal transformations, the development of 3:12 Transformation Ministries and the writing of *3:12 Transformation*, the book—friends who have shared with us, strengthened us, and prayed with us in everyday life. We are positive this was God's hand guiding His message into the hearts and lives of others who will protect and love 3:12 Transformation and God's message, just as we have. I am honored to acknowledge some of those friends at this time.

Doug Cullett: There was a season in my life when you were the only human I knew who could give me any hope for the future. Thank you, my friend, for your words and kindness.

Pastor Tom Zobrist: You were the vessel God chose to reveal the power of truth through Jesus Christ for my spiritual eyes to see. Thank you for your obedience to God's calling in your life and your faith in seeing Teresa and me as God's victory, not just casualties of this world.

Pastor Jeff and Monna Rasanen: God promises us shepherds to lead His sheep and tend His flocks. My family is truly blessed that you, Pastor Jeff, are one of the shepherds God has provided. I also am grateful in Christ for you as my friend and thankful for all the support and encouragement you have given this ministry and my spirit! Monna, thank you for being an example of love, gentleness, and encouragement not only for Teresa to know but for all the other women you influence for Christ. We love you both.

Larry Shonk: God pointed me to you early on when developing the vision of 3:12 Transformation into a ministry. Thank you, my brother, for your spiritual insight, wisdom, and vision and for being my partner in ministry and friend in life.

Pastor Larry and Linda McKinney: Thank you both for your hearts for Jesus. You are the example of Christ that the entire world needs to see. We have been blessed by your friendship and the opportunities God has presented through it. Praise God for you both!

Our church family at Faith Assembly of God, Elk Run Heights, Iowa: Thank you all for your support, encouragement, prayers, time spent together and above all, your love. The Lord may have called us out of your physical midst, but our spirits are with you always. You are such a precious gift from the Lord and have been instrumental in our faith. We love you very dearly and praise God we are part of the family of faith.

Mike and Kathy Smith: You have been the most encouraging friends Teresa and I could have ever been blessed to receive. Your faith has strengthened ours on numerous occasions and through numerous trials. Through our friendship, I have realized God has brought us together to share His message with the multitudes, but we always take the time to share His love with each other first. Thank you for your hearts and faith and ongoing encouragement with which you fill our lives. We love you.

To my mother-in law, Mary, and my fathers-in law, Terry and Lemmy: Thank you for your kindness and support throughout life. Never once was I judged; even at the height of my selfishness and sin, you all remained family, with love and support for your daughter's choice. Thank you so much.

My siblings, Deanna, Bob, Lee, Jerry, Troy: Thank you for your acceptance and kindness toward me throughout my entire life. You are all my brothers and sisters in Christ as well as this world.

My mother, Judy Ioerger: I have learned much from you throughout my life, Mother, and now I see more clearly than ever before by God's grace. Thank you for always loving me and always believing that God had a plan. I thank our heavenly Father that I can give back a fraction of the love that you have shown me. Love you, Mom.

To my children and grandchildren: I thank God for the opportunity to be your worldly father. I would like to acknowledge how you have encouraged me to be a better man and to lead you all with faith. Jesus is the way, the truth, and the life, my children and grandchildren. No matter what I leave any of you in this life, if I leave you an example of faith and trust in Jesus Christ, I will have left you riches beyond measure. Acknowledge the Lord each day, and He will acknowledge you for eternity! I love you, my children.

Teresa, my wife: God blessed me more than I could repay the day I met you. When different pastors first spoke over us and said our best days were yet to come, my heart rejoiced in hope and belief. Thank you, my love, for sharing the reality of that proclamation come to pass with me. I love you more each day, Teresa. Thank you for standing by me when the world told you to run. Thank you for your love and faith. I love you, Teresa.

Introduction

To begin with, I must give praise and thanks to my God and Savior Jesus Christ, without whom I would never have had the courage, faith, and love to dream of writing a book about overcoming addictions and a life burdened with shame, guilt, and despair.

Father, thank You! I pray the words in this book may give hope and faith where once there was despair and doubt. May these words give peace to lost souls who once knew only anxiety and chaos. May this book bring courage and confidence to those who have known only fear and worthlessness. Above all, Father, may the words on these pages give glory and praise to Your Son, Jesus Christ, and magnify Your holy name. May this book be an offering to You, God. May it give insight to Your true love and mercy for all those who seek Your forgiveness. May this book deliver the answer to so many of Your lost children who have sought to find the cure while entangled in sin and burdened in bondage of addictions; those who have always tried to fill their hearts with expectations of the world as opposed to Your indescribable love. Father, I will reveal myself through these pages in an attempt to let all those who read them have their eyes opened and their hearts convicted by the revealing of Your Holy Spirit. My prayer would be that those who read this book will undoubtedly identify that the only true antidote to a broken life is the surrendering of oneself and accepting Your Son's sacrifice of love and forgiveness. May the words echo through the hearts of those who read them and shatter all chains of bondage that have restrained them from Your great love. May the once-fearful lost soul You have so mercifully chosen to spread this message truly express the transformation of a new life in Jesus Christ. May this transformation be spread throughout Your creation. Through the power of Your Holy Spirit, I pray You bring forth many more transformations for Your glory. And Father, let those who read believe!

The 3:12 Transformation was a vision communicated to me through a dream by the Holy Spirit of God on November 29, 2010. God placed a calling upon my heart for a recovery program that established 100 percent focus and credit toward Jesus Christ. Being an alcoholic who struggled with life for more than twenty years, my heart was convicted that without Jesus Christ and the guidance of the Holy Spirit, I would never obtain true, joyous sobriety. In my dream, I spoke to another man in recovery. I shared the burden upon my heart that if people would prioritize Jesus first and seek God with all their hearts, the rest of the issues would also be resolved. I said to him, "Lives would be saved, marriages put back together, and children spared from the same brokenness as their parents." He said to me, *"You know what to do!"* Immediately, I woke up, looking directly at the alarm clock on my nightstand. The time was 3:12 a.m. I felt wide awake. I felt as if a spiritual presence had communicated to me, a presence of knowledge, wisdom, guidance, authority, power, and tremendous love. The thought, *3:12 Transformation*, came to my mind and out of my lips before I could even collect any of my own thoughts. I rose from bed, and I felt I was led to look at the gospel of John 3:12. I grabbed my Bible from the dresser and hurried into the kitchen, turned to the gospel of John, chapter 3, verse 12, and read,

"If you do not believe when I have told you earthly things, how will you believe when I tell you Heavenly things?" (John 3:12).

Those were the words Jesus spoke to Nicodemus while talking with him on the subject of rebirth in the Holy Spirit. I can't explain the overwhelming energy, love, peace, and faith that ran through my spirit when I read the verse to which I believed God was directly pointing me. It had happened—the Lord truly spoke to me, plainly and clearly. I realized that the dream was not an ordinary dream; it was a message the Lord delivered to me! This message confirmed the calling and desire of my heart to see a ministry that focused on Jesus Christ and God's love from start to finish. I spent some time in prayer and thankfulness, and finally, I returned to sleep well after 5: 00 a.m. I would have been more than convinced with the dream and the verse I read from John 3:12, but the Lord had just begun to open my eyes with what He had in store for me to see and the true weight of the message He had revealed to me through the vision. Later that morning, I felt I was led to go through all the chapter-3-verse-12s in the Bible. My wife and I discovered it was a God-divine message that put the verses of the Bible into action, which would lead souls out of bondage and disparity of life and into transformational truth and spiritual rebirth. It showed us of God's great love for us—His mercy and patience, His understanding, His encouragement, His calling and the power He will give us, His promise of peace and joy in this life, and His promise of our eternal life with Him in heaven.

The 3:12 Transformation is a four-phase application of spiritual rebirth: surrender, believe, live, and proclaim. It contains twenty-six chapter-3-verse-12 excerpts from the Bible. After twenty years of attempting to overcome alcoholism, I realized that not drinking was merely a fraction of the underlying problems. Yes, we all have heard this before: What do you have when you sober up a drunken horse thief? The answer: you still have a horse thief! But something resonated deeper in my soul. I began to see that conforming, functioning, and succeeding in life was an understanding I had been given through my own expectations and the standards of others. The same inner strength and voice that was telling me the world's standards were not the guarantee to happiness also was leading me to much more than what the world has to offer. I had been searching for true peace, forgiveness, and confidence that my failures would not be repeated.

Now, before you read another sentence, I assure you that I am not perfect, nor do I ever expect to be in this world. However, I will share with you the peace and trust I have received through the true surrender of giving my life to Jesus Christ. I will tell you the circumstances Christ has overcome for me. I will tell you of hope, faith, and my relationship with the Creator of the universe that I never thought possible! I also will tell you that God longs for that same relationship with you! We are not struggling merely with addictions or life circumstances that have shifted all things out of balance by their own power; circumstances that can be conquered and laid to rest through our willpower and individual strength. We are prisoners of sin. We are prisoners of a poverty mentality and a self-esteem identity crisis. God will not only set you free; He will burst the chains from you and take you on a journey with His Son into freedom and liberty. Your true identity will be claimed again through the living Word of God that penetrates your soul and mind! I will explain to you, in my humble terms, 3:12 Transformation. I will describe the way my heart felt when it was explained to me through God's guidance and use of the Scriptures. This book, *3:12 Transformation*, at first seemed obviously designed for the alcoholic and addict. But we have discovered that the outlined transformation and program will work for any life that has not known Jesus Christ or has turned away at some point. The 3:12 Transformation will lead people to Christ and freedom!

I originally wrote and submitted *3:12 Transformation* for publication in June 2012. The Lord has placed it upon my heart to write a second edition. This edition will maintain the main content and theme of the original *3:12 Transformation* book, with the addition of some new content and revelation the Lord has placed upon my heart and spirit while being part of the ministry. Since its inception, 3:12 Transformation Ministries has spread to several churches throughout Iowa, as well as to county jails and state prisons. We have been blessed and humbled to see the mighty works the Lord has done with this ministry in a short time. God has freed many men and women and called them into service and ministry as a result.

As you read *3:12 Transformation*, I would ask you to go at a pace that best suits your personal need. The book itself is not a burdensome read or overly lengthy. I would hope the effect and depth of God's words and guidance last a lifetime and launch you into a newfound optimism and resolve for whatever road may be placed before you. *3:12 Transformation* is meant to engage the reader and give each individual an opportunity for God's Spirit to reveal new insight, love, promises, and hope. The questions at the end of each chapter are meant to be answered by the reader. I strongly urge you to take the time to read the Scripture verses discussed throughout the book and relate them to how they fit with your life and speak to you. Be transparent and honest when answering these questions, and make them the deepest thoughts of your heart and mind. *3:12 Transformation* was never meant merely to be W. L. Ioerger's transformational story; it is meant to be our entire story. Take time in prayer with our heavenly Father and get as much out of His words as you can. Come back and visit this book as time passes to compare your thoughts and prayers with your future mind-set, and see the magnificent work the Lord will have done in your life. I can say I attend 3:12 Transformation Ministries meetings and groups several times weekly. I never cease to be amazed by how God uses the verses and my life's current situations to further guide me. He reveals new wisdom, touches me with His love and, when need be, convicts my heart to steer me on His straight path once again.

We all come from different backgrounds and circumstances. Some of us may carry the burden of being the cause of great misery and pain, while others may feel as though they have been the recipient of greatly unjust treatment. We are all sinners who need salvation. Don't look back along the way; you do not want to miss a single minute of what God has in store for you.

May the peace of the Lord fill your hearts as you read this message and a mighty work be performed through your spirit, by God's grace and mercy bestowed upon you.

Surrender

Chapter 1

Surrender the Fight

Blame

Then the man said, "The woman whom You gave to be with me,
she gave me of the tree, and I ate."—Genesis 3:12

Blame is fitting, to begin with, for the simple fact that it usually leads to surrender. We like to blame everyone around us for why we fall so short. We blame the circumstances in which we are involved for life being out of control. We blame God for creating us as we are or for placing us in uncontrollable situations. Blame is the beginning of selfish justification of ourselves and our actions. Blame can also be used as a fear blanket to protect us from being held accountable or dealing with issues that are unpleasant. It is much easier to sweep our shortcomings under the rug than expose the mess for ourselves and others to see.

Blame is a denial of accountability that can lead our consciences and hearts to deeper and darker levels of hardening. This is usually not realized, however, by the alcoholic or addict. To be honest, it is usually not realized by most of the human race. We confirm our own worst fears when we accept responsibility for mistakes. We confirm our inability to control all things.

We sink into depression when we give thought to what we view as our failures. After all, we are unworthy and not good enough—we know this, but we don't want the rest of the world discovering our secrets. I was constantly angry and afraid the entire world, friends, and loved ones thought that way about me already, but I was bound and determined to prove them wrong.

Then there is another form of blame: the soul of desperation that blames itself for every single problem that arises and the individual who stops blaming himself or herself only when under the influence of alcohol, drugs, or any obsessive lifestyle that enables wiping away his or her conscience for a short time. Both versions of blame are dangerous and unhealthy, and each will lead to a boiling point where the human spirit has to be forgiven of its hypocrisy or plunge itself into selfish actions of sin to temporarily relieve the pain. It seems as though we long to condemn ourselves and others once the wheel of blame starts to spin. Our souls begin preparing and condoning our actions that will follow, as a self-pitying appetite refusing to be satisfied.

In Genesis 3:12, we see the first human created on earth use the self-denial mechanism of blame. Adam claims he merely ate the fruit Eve gave him. He also blames God for being the one to give him Eve—that is a further attempt to remove himself from responsibility for his actions. As a result, Adam and Eve are made to leave the garden of Eden. Does blame not spiral? From the fall of Adam and Eve, all mankind has been placed in a position of having to seek God, rather than walk with Him. What if Adam had said, "Lord, I have done wrong! I was selfish and disobeyed You. Please forgive me"? What if we took responsibility for our mistakes and sins long before we reached the point of brokenness and removal from our garden of Eden? What if we could surrender blame and the need to justify or condemn ourselves constantly before we reached the point of no return? Unfortunately, we are too fearful, prideful, and selfish to point the blame where it needs to be. The blame lies in the lack of our relationship with God and our selfish removal of His presence in our hearts.

In my last bout of alcoholism, there was a slow wave of blame that manifested into a major tsunami by the end. I was trying to be the man I always felt I needed to be. I had a very good job, along with a wonderful wife who stood by me through past trials, which was nothing short of a miracle in itself. We had four healthy children, a nice home, and financially, we had come through a rough season but were looking forward to brighter days ahead. We enjoyed a loving and supportive family, and we spent time together as often as possible. We also had become members of a local church for the first time in our lives and attended almost every Sunday. There was no excuse for the events that followed to ever take place. Well, actually there was. Once again, I began to obsess over details, timelines, and expectations that I felt needed to be met. I attempted to control every aspect of life—the amount of money we made, how much we should have in the bank, how our children should act, the hours each day I spent in my garden and in my career, etc. These obsessions came about very slowly and well disguised but were there nonetheless. As I allowed myself to be more engulfed in my own righteousness, I began to blame circumstances for unmet expectations. I also blamed others for their lack of discipline and commitment. I truly became a self-proclaimed judge of everything and everyone around me. Then there were bouts of the other extreme, when I blamed myself for not measuring up to expectations and blamed others for being created perfectly while I was a worthless lump of humanity. I finally realized that I could not control the promotion I felt I deserved at work or the fixing of my children that I thought was needed.

The financial situation was not at all where I felt it should be, and I believed that was due to my own foolish spending and inability to earn enough. I started to let the feelings of worthlessness and despair set in. As a result, I began to drink again in a concealed manner and when confronted, I lied about doing it. Then, of course, all the shame and guilt, from which I'd never felt freed, returned from the past, along with the new failure and misery I was embarking upon. I became resentful of who I was, of the people around me, and that God had placed me in this position again. I truly hated myself. I faced a war within myself at all times. The only mechanism available to me for peace was to drink, which would start the vicious cycle all over again. I wanted peace and success more than anything else in the world. I longed for an answer. At this time in my life, I had little to no relationship with Jesus Christ. I'd had plenty of religion throughout my life but no true relationship with Christ to speak of.

I was in need of a spiritual overhaul but had no foundation upon which to build to take the steps needed. I couldn't possibly ask for help; that would make my own convictions of worthlessness official. All I knew to do at the time was continue to fight by my own means and hope I would somehow fix the situation. I, however, simply made matters worse. My drinking increased, along with blaming everything and everyone in my life. Through my repetitive blame, lack of hope, and self-hatred, my heart and mind were convinced of my personal worthlessness. My soul had preapproved any coming behavior, no matter how destructive or selfish. I was entitled to feel the way I did.

I became thoroughly intoxicated one afternoon and went home to Teresa and our children and informed them I was not worthy of the marriage. I thought I was setting them free to pursue happiness in life. I would merely be in their way and was no more than a worthless alcoholic. I also informed Teresa I would be pursuing another woman. You see, when I had reached my point of throwing in the towel, my blinded mind and soul only viewed my selfishness and what could be used to fulfill some sort of physical and mental relief. I was concerned for my wife and children, their future, and the shame this would cause them, but—let's be honest about the situation—the number-one person I was really concerned about was me. At that point in my thought process, alcohol was the only means to happiness because it would drown out any feelings of remorse and guilt that haunted any sober moment. And how do we feel value and worth when we question if we have any? I would seek that self-value based on what others were willing to do for me and with me. I could not identify that any individual willing to boost my ego at such a time was just as lost and desolate as I! My plan was to stay under the influence of alcohol and, eventually, any drug needed to control the situation of doom and gloom. I planned to finish out my days under the societal disguise: "Well, he was always a good guy, but the booze got the better of him." The truth was, I wasn't a good guy, and I knew it.

You can only imagine the shock this was to my family. As I said, I had been hiding things and warring within myself. Blame had become my partner in sin. Blame had allowed me to place all my selfish actions on the hearts of my family. I hated myself. I blamed myself. I blamed God. Complete despair and lost hope became the anchors that held my life's foundation firmly in the pit of mental hell.

Question Our Existence

> Why did the knees receive me? Or why the
> breasts, that I should nurse?—Job 3:12

7

In this verse, Job is asking why he was ever born. Job had just gone through loss of family, possessions, friends, and all status in the world that he had attained. Job also was afflicted with physical, mental, and emotional sickness and suffering. How many of us have felt the same as Job at one time or another in life?

The next morning, I awoke and realized what my drinking and selfish life had cost my family and me. I stared at the wall in disbelief and shock. Was this the course of my life? Was all the nurturing from childhood, training from schools, and lessons in life merely ways to pass time, leading up to complete moral bankruptcy? Did my mother nurse me when I was young and my father make sure I always was fed and clothed and had a bed to sleep in for me to simply become an evil monster who would be used to destroy other loved ones' lives? Were Teresa and my children supposed to accept my betrayal and selfish addiction and go on with their lives abandoned? I couldn't believe life had led me to this newfound bottom of emotional torture once again. I saw the pain in my wife's eyes. I felt the betrayal I had caused her each time I looked at her innocent face. I saw the abandonment in my children's faces. I felt they looked upon their father with disgust, anger, and fear. I had crushed all their dreams, securities, and sense of family. I wished I had never been born. My hate for myself grew stronger by the minute. Why did God let me destroy all that was precious to me? It was bad enough to waste my own life, but why did I have to ruin my wife's and children's lives as well? I sunk into the deepest depression and fear I had ever known in my life. I longed for death. I felt pain and anxiety with every breath that entered my chest. I was daydreaming about ways to vanish and never hurt anyone or myself again. It seemed my life had been a blur; as though I were a spectator in the crazy events that led to this moment, caught completely by surprise and shocked by what had happened, hoping and praying it was only a dream but soberly realizing I was awake.

All the feelings leading up to the events—the ones where I felt as though my only peace and calm would be attained through alcohol—were dramatically removed and replaced with utter isolation, fear, and loneliness.

Like Job, I stood to lose my family, possessions, and all that remained of my positive reputation. I was also in the midst of mental and emotional distress and physically was a wreck. Unlike Job, I had brought this upon myself and my family. I carried all the guilt, shame, and resentment on my own soul. I so longed for release and peace from the burden I had acquired throughout my selfish life. I longed for that release to the point of contemplating suicide. My thoughts of suicide lasted several days. The anxiety I felt during this time was complete around-the-clock misery. I could not make my mind focus on anything other than my horrible addiction and actions. I would close my eyes while driving to see how long it would be before I ran off the road or into a telephone pole or building. I just couldn't seem to go long enough without the thoughts of injuring innocent people, so I would open my eyes just in time to hit the brakes or swerve back onto the road. Then, I shifted toward thoughts of overdosing on pills or possibly cutting my wrists. Finally, I planned to shoot myself and was occupied much of the time with how I would do it. My religious upbringing had convinced me that suicide would firmly plant my eternity in hell, so I decided I would give myself time to confess any sins after the fact and just before death. I had several firearms in my house and had chosen my trusty 12-gauge to be the instrument. I even planned to perform the deed under our apple tree, which stood at the north end of our garden. I didn't want to hurt anyone, but I did wish to see people mourn my death and realize how sorry I was for my actions. I figured when Teresa and my loved ones saw me under the apple tree, they would acknowledge just how sorry I was and how much I truly loved them. Only by God's grace were these actions not carried out. I remember on one night in particular, only God's protection could have been the reason I did not unlock the gun cabinet and follow through with the plans of lost hope I had conceived. I went three days without food. I could not bring myself to eat, nor did I desire to eat. I drank water or coffee only, and the thought of food made my stomach turn. It was as if there was a power greater than me pressuring me to admit defeat, bow out of the human race, and end my pain and the pain of my loved ones.

The human spirit can only withstand so much misery before it will break. I was at that breaking point. One afternoon, on my way home from work, I had a discussion with God that changed my life forever. I was sure my marriage was over, my children had written me off, and I was destined to be a drunk 'til my dying day. I did not wish that to be my destiny. I cried out to God to forgive me. I confessed my sins and selfish life. I openly told God that I was guilty of turning away from Him. I yelled out, "God, fix me or kill me!" My entire being was involved in that request. My spirit groaned for peace and forgiveness. I was willing to accept any form of correction God had in store for me. I also asked God to take care of Teresa and my children, no matter what His decision was for me. I said I was a child of His, the true God. I was a child of light, not darkness. I prayed to God to deliver me from the evil and temptation of which I had been guilty in life. I asked God to deliver me and my family and claim us as His children. I rebuked the Devil and begged God to forever drive him out of my life. Little did I know the answer God was about to give. At this time, I was given a small mustard seed of faith. I was not sure why, other than God's intervention, but there was a fraction of hope and peace I had not known before that moment. God gave me just enough faith and courage to recognize that maybe He loved me after all. I thought, *God has not removed me from the face of the earth up to this point. Why hasn't He?*

God Loves Us

For whom the Lord loves He corrects, just as a father
the son in whom he delights. —Proverbs 3:12

After crying out to God for His forgiveness and help, a change began
to take place within me. I truly had a revelation that God loved
me. This was the first of a few revelations God gave me that would
forever change my life and the direction of it. Now, to be fair, I must
admit that this change, however positive, was very small at that time.
But don't miss the main point: it was a change—and a change for
the positive! I felt a sense of peace. I felt that I was loved, that love
was coming through my spirit from God. I did not understand it at
that time, but I wanted to know more about this hope and comfort
I was sensing.

This new feeling had not been my normal outlook on God. I had
always viewed God as a wise, judgmental, white-bearded power that
sat upon a throne in the clouds, looking down upon creation, shaking
His head at our lack of religion. I believed God to be so unreachable
that I could hardly imagine His dissatisfaction with my life and what
I had chosen to do with it. I knew Jesus was the Son of God; He came
to earth, died, and rose again on the third day. I also believed that
whatever it was that Jesus had done for me, I was not worthy of it. I
believed I was too damaged to have a close relationship with God,
let alone be counted worthy of forgiveness. I felt ashamed of who
I was and what I had done, and I was nowhere close to measuring
up to God's expectations of me. Why wouldn't I have this outlook of
God? After all, I had lived all my life feeling unlovable, unwanted,
unworthy, and not equal to others. My experiences with God had
been one religious expectation after another of God's awesome
power that left me with the impression I was a disappointment. I
mean, God had done so much for me, yet I did not return the respect

11

and discipline needed to be counted worthy. My desires of God were portrayed through the rituals of man and a sacrifice of time once per week at church. I did not recognize that my heart was longing for so much more interaction with God. I did not even know that the hole in my soul that I had been trying to fill all my life was the absence of my relationship with God.

How often has this world and man-made traditions stood between us and the furthering of our relationship with God? Our religious leadership may tell us to make a particular sacrifice that we may not necessarily understand at the time. We are told to commit our lives to God at a certain age, when we are in no way able or truly prepared to perform the commitment we are making. We are brought up in a repetitive, routine, and stagnant religion. Now, there is no rule that says religion has to be exciting and fun all the time, but isn't it worth it to put some sense of emotion toward our eternal souls? Don't worry; I'm not resorting to blame again. I am merely stating that the reason my religious beliefs never led me to a relationship with God, other than unworthiness, was because I sought religion and not God. I looked at man's traditions and expectations as religious beliefs. I did not look at God's heart and desire for intimacy with me through His Word. That's where I came to understand that through the prayer I cried out in voice and spirit that day in my truck, God responded directly to me out of love.

At this time, I began to read the Bible on my own for the first time in my life, in an attempt to confirm that feeling I had received. God answered me through the pages that I read. I went right to the New Testament and started with the gospel of Matthew. I began to see, time and time again, the love God has for us. John 3:16 is the greatest verse contained in the Bible to prove this love:

"For God so loved the world that He gave His only begotten Son, that whoever believes in Him should not perish but have everlasting life."

Proverbs 3:12 tells us that God does indeed love us, not only as a God-to-creation relationship but as a father-to-son relationship. We see that God delights in our correction through Him. Correction, in the sense of a father-and-son relationship, is based upon love and hope that the son will grow, strengthen, and know the fullness of life. This is exactly what God wants for each one of us. God delights in our correction because it will lead us directly to Him in a more intimate relationship. God has our attention when we are truly broken. When we reach the point of desperation and have lost hope for anything joyful, we are open to suggestions and advice. How often did we accept advice before we reached our sense of doom? In my own experience, I can honestly say I seldom listened to any advice while in my selfish life of addiction and chaos. If God truly loves us as a father loves a son, then that makes us His child. Would a loving father ever abandon his child? Wouldn't a loving father give his child the correction, support, and tools needed to help him succeed and to right the wrongs he has done? At times, our Father may let us travel headfirst into the brick wall we are bound and determined to crash into, in order to let us come to that place of surrender. Once we finally impact, however, who is the first one to help us back up? Who gives us the courage to try again? Who tells us what we need to change and what we need to build upon? It is always our loving Father. That loving Father just so happens to be the Creator of the universe and all contained therein. God is our loving Father, and He loves each and every one of us with a passion and pureness we can only imagine.

When we first ask God into our lives and confess our sins, God's Spirit sings for joy. The angels sing and praise in heaven, and there is rejoicing throughout (Luke 15:7, 10). The parable of the prodigal son (Luke 15:11–32) best explains the relationship our heavenly Father longs to have with us. This parable tells how the father of the prodigal son sees the son coming from a long distance off and runs to meet him. The father then embraces him, kisses him, and orders preparations be made to throw a feast to celebrate the return of the son.

The father does not run out to him and say, "Ha! I told you that you were making a big mistake, but you wouldn't listen. See? You should have listened to me to begin with, you foolish son! You are going to have to work this off, and I am not going to forget it any time soon."

That parable is for us to visualize God's response to us when we return to Him in faith and repentance. We all have played the prodigal son at one time or another, but our Father runs to meet us even when we are still a long way off and rejoices at our return!

Another example of God's great love for us comes from Ephesians:

"For we are His workmanship, created in Christ Jesus for good works, which God prepared beforehand that we should walk in them" (Ephesians 2:10).

The following story was inspired by Pastor Jeff Rasanen.

In Ephesians 2:10, the word "workmanship" in Greek translation is "masterpiece," for we are God's masterpiece! Imagine a priceless painting by a renowned artist—Picasso, Rembrandt. The painting holds great value and is priceless to the eyes of the collector seeking the painting. Somewhere along the way, the painting ends up misplaced, misused, or misunderstood. It is set aside and eventually thrown in the trash with the belief it has no value. The collector comes along and sees the painting in the trash. Immediately, he recognizes the value, worth, and masterpiece that it truly is. He removes the masterpiece and rejoices because he has found it! He doesn't see the dirt and blemishes or the work needed to restore the masterpiece. He only sees the great value it holds in his eyes and the beautiful work of art it is. He is willing to do anything to save and restore his masterpiece ... no matter the cost.

We are that masterpiece! God is the collector. God sees past all our faults, dirt, and sin. God rejoices that He has found us, and His plan for restoration can begin. He spared no cost to save His masterpiece ... that is why He sent His Son, Jesus Christ, to provide the payment.

If God does not love us with such passion, why is the enemy of God, Satan, so determined to steal our souls away from Him? The human soul is precious and extremely valuable to God. When we begin to surrender our lives to God, we will feel some peace and relief from the anguish we have known. This peace is our spirits desperately reaching out to the Spirit of God and receiving a response, begging for forgiveness, longing for comfort, and clinging to a shred of hope that God can and will correct us.

When I first felt the presence and love of God, it was as if my inner spirit had received the thirst-quenching drink it had so longed for. My eyes watered with tears of joy. I felt a weight fall from my soul, and there was a sense that everything would be okay. I actually felt as though I was in the loving protection of my God, and He would keep me safe when the world only left me desolate. I ceased torturing myself and thanked God for life. God was beginning the transformation of His child, whom He loved. The courts of heaven rejoiced with angelic harmony.

God does love you. The Bible tells us again and again of His love for us. No matter what you have done in life and how far away you have drifted from God, He will forgive you. God will correct you, redeem you, and give you joy. Be patient and enjoy this newfound love God has shown you. With the feeling of true love and purposeful correction from God, we can begin to see more clearly His wisdom and the path on which we are to walk. Dedicate your heart and soul to God and His Word. Give as much time as possible to the Bible, and watch the writings of God come to life in your spirit.

Blame

Have you used blame throughout your life? Give circumstances where you have blamed others, yourself, or God.

_____

_____

_____

_____

_____

_____

_____

_____

_____

_____

_____

_____

_____

_____

_____

Look at the following Bible verses and describe how they relate to blame: Numbers 21:5; 1 Samuel 22:13–18; Isaiah 40:27; John 5:7.

_____

_____

_____

_____

_____

_____

_____

_____

_____

_____

_____

If you currently are a Christian, what are you blaming that is keeping you from living a life as a true disciple of Jesus Christ?

_____

_____

_____

_____

_____

_____

_____

_____

_____

_____

_____

_____

Question Our Existence

Have you experienced a time where you questioned why you were ever born or longed to disappear, even considering death as your option?

_____

_____

_____

_____

_____

_____

_____

_____

_____

_____

Look at the following Bible verses and share how they relate to questioning your existence: Numbers 11:14–15; 1 Kings 19:4; Jonah 4:8; Job 6:11–13.

_____

_____

_____

_____

_____

_____

_____

_____

_____

_____

At times, it is easy to question our purpose and reason for life, as well as our reason for being a Christian. At times, we lose hope and try to cling to our mentality that tells us the world would be better off without us in it. Do you ever have those moments?

_____
_____
_____
_____
_____
_____
_____
_____
_____
_____

God Loves Us

Do you believe God truly loves you? Are you willing to accept His love, guidance, and correction in your life?

_____
_____
_____
_____
_____
_____
_____
_____
_____
_____

Look at the following Bible verses and share how they speak to you on God's love and correction: Jeremiah 10:24; Jeremiah 29:11; John 3:17; Romans 5:8; Romans 6:23; 2 Corinthians 6:2; 2 Timothy 3:16; 1 Peter 5:6–7; Hebrews 12:6; 1 John 3:16.

_____

_____

_____

_____

_____

_____

_____

_____

_____

_____

_____

_____

Chapter 2

God Knows What Is Best

I know that nothing is better for them than to
rejoice, and to do good in their lives.
—Ecclesiastes 3:12

Once we begin to acknowledge and believe that God truly loves us, we are willing to surrender and learn more about that love. Our mood and demeanor seems a bit more stable, and we lose some of the selfish "me, me, me" attitude. We can see outside of ourselves for the first time and focus on God and loved ones and attempting to serve them. This is a radical change of heart for the individual who has been lost in his or her own selfishness through addictions and sin. You may ask, "Is this by our own resources or intelligence?" Not at all. God knows exactly what is needed to begin molding His children into the loving, obedient servants He has chosen and created them to be.

Ecclesiastes 3:12 tells us to rejoice and do good. It goes as far as telling us nothing is better for us than rejoicing and doing good! That is quite a statement God wants us to hear. Why the strong emphasis on these two actions? The answer is simple yet powerful. We are coming out of a life of personal and worldly condemnation, of circumstances that have given us little reason to collect a positive thought, let alone rejoice—circumstances such as years of substance abuse, depression, divorce, prison, joblessness, attempted suicide, family abandonment, loss of loved ones ... the list goes on. We have been an ocean of doubts and disappointments. Our minds and spirits have been the main chains of bondage that have restrained us from any hope of happiness. Our deeds and actions have been a direct result of what our minds had been: negative and ungodly. God wants us to start seeing our lives and His presence with us in a completely different light. We need to let God transform our minds and spirits into the creation He made us to be.

"But you are a chosen people, a royal priesthood, a holy nation, God's special possession, that you may declare the praises of Him who called you out of darkness into His wonderful light" (1 Peter 2:9).

This begins with the ability to identify the blessings God has bestowed upon us and share those blessings with others. God has given us much to be thankful for. Most of us have some sort of family, support, or loved ones who never turned their backs on us, even during our darkest times. We have our beautiful world God has created and given for our lives and enjoyment. We have God's holy words and promises to give us encouragement. We have been given salvation and forgiveness. Most of all, we have the love of our Creator, who longs to have a personal relationship with us. We are at a stage where we can truly recognize and appreciate the little things in life, the things that once seemed little, but we can now rejoice in how big they truly are. As we further read the Bible and uncover God's Word, we see the overwhelming evidence that God wants us joyful and happy, not only in heaven with Him one day but in this present life as well. As we begin to become more positive and thankful, we find our new mentality taking over from our negative thought process that brought us to our demise in previous attempts.

Never underestimate the power of a thankful attitude. A thankful attitude leads to giving and helping. We are so accustomed to feeling sorry for ourselves. We have always dwelled upon how much better everyone else's life was than ours. We complained about our circumstances, how the world mistreated us, and our inability to get a break like everyone else. We selfishly sought to further fill our worldly desires without being thankful for what we had been given. At times, we have been the perfect example of a three-year-old child in a grocery store, throwing a fit over not getting what we grabbed and tossed in the cart. Why would anyone give an ounce of energy to help us when we were trapped in that mind-set? It was all about us, for us, and owed to us! We must get some humility and joy into our minds, which will slowly chase out the selfish corruption of sin in which we have dwelt.

Here are a couple of very important points that need to be discussed at this time:

1. It is crucial to get plugged into a loving church family.
2. Don't let the Enemy steal your joy.

My wife and I made the commitment to serve God as best we could. We surrendered our lives and asked God to guide us by His Spirit and fill us with joy and peace. In return, God brought us into a true church family. A church family is not the same as a building where like-minded members of the same denomination meet once a week for their obligated time with the Lord. We entered a set of doors where the people inside welcomed us immediately with open arms. They hugged us, shook our hands, and asked us our reason for being there, and we were invited to dinner by three different couples that first day. Those couples are still inviting us to dinner and are as sincere today as they were the first day we met. Through those acquaintances we have found true friends who will encourage us, pray for us, hold us accountable, and discuss all things pertaining to our lives, individually and as a couple. Most important, they taught us how to truly rejoice! Our pastor, Jeff, and his wife, Monna, encouraged us to get involved and help those less fortunate. They took the time to counsel us to grow us in Christ. Above all, they taught us to rejoice in the Lord and His goodness. God will put us in contact with those who will strengthen us in His name. Spend the time and go church-shopping. Find the church that truly is an example of a family, one that will share your hopes and dreams and always listen to your fears and concerns. Also, find one that is willing to put you to work for the good of the whole church family. It is important to feel we are giving back some of the joy with which God has blessed us. Many people claim they can have a perfectly good relationship with God without attending church or being involved with a church family. Whether that is or is not true, I need a church family filled with like-minded people who can give encouragement and support to my family. Also, it is my responsibility to give encouragement and support to others within my church family. Once again, it is not all about us anymore. That was the old, selfish mentality, where it was very comfortable to say fellowshipping with other like-minded Christians was unnecessary. The old mentality needs to go, and the new God mentality must replace it.

"And let us consider one another in order to stir up love and good works, not forsaking the assembling of ourselves together, as is the manner of some, but exhorting one another, and so much the more as you see the Day approaching" (Hebrews 10:24–25).

Beware of the Enemy. If you think for one single minute Satan will sit back and admit defeat, you are seriously wrong. You are beginning to sense God's spirit and peace. You are rejoicing in what God has given you and wishing to perform good works for God and others. You are no longer a sideliner in the kingdom of God; you are becoming a player. Satan will come after you with new trials and old memories. Satan attempted to sway Jesus Christ Himself from His mission, as we see in the Gospels (Matthew 4:1–11; Luke 4:1–13). Do you think he won't come after you? Satan hates you. He wants to separate you from God again. That is what you were before surrendering your life to God—separated. Expect any and every little thing that can go wrong to go wrong. Expect bouts of negative thoughts, where you try to slip into your past and doubt that you can continue on this new journey. Do not be moved when others doubt you and try to condemn you again for past mistakes. God has forgiven you for all your transgressions. Don't let Satan deceive you into thinking you're not forgiven.

With what do you choose to be consumed? You will be an image and reflection of what you choose to let consume you. If you choose to be consumed by selfishness, fear, doubt, worry, greed, lust, addictions, etc., you will be the reflection of that person who is led by such actions. If you are consumed by the perceptions of who you think you should be and who the world says you need to be, you will reflect a worldly person, consumed by your selfishness and anxiety, to live up to those expectations. You will be the image of one all alone to face the world.

That being said, if you choose to be consumed by the promises of Jesus Christ, what will happen? If you choose to be consumed with the joy of salvation in Christ, forgiveness and grace from God, and obedience to the teachings of God's Word ... you will reflect the image of a person who is joyous in his or her salvation, forgiven and forgiving, and eager to spread his or her salvation and good news to others who also may want salvation. You will be the image of one who is confident that he or she will never be forsaken, forgotten, or orphaned.

Our thoughts are our own choices. We can listen to God's spirit, which bestows peace and love, or we can be prisoners to the attacks of the Enemy that are doubt and fear. The following is a key Scripture to remember and use as defense when the negative thoughts try to enter your mind:

"For God has not given us a spirit of fear, but of power and of love and of sound mind" (2 Timothy 1:7).

Listen closely to the words of 2 Timothy 1:7 and recognize what they are saying. God has not forgiven us our sins and past lives to be trapped by regrets and resentments. God has not granted us salvation and promised us His Spirit to again be fearful of our past or our future. God has given us a new Spirit. God's Spirit brings forth peace, love, and the power of the Holy Spirit—these three things! If our minds are occupied anywhere other than God's peace, love, or power, we can identify that it is not of God. If not of God, then where is it coming from? The Enemy, Satan, once again is up to his old tricks, trying to separate our thoughts and hearts from the Lord. As you catch yourself, remember: how did Jesus combat these attacks? He spoke Scripture to the Enemy and commanded him, "Get behind Me, Satan" (Luke 4:8).

We have the same authority to command the Enemy out of our minds and choose to focus on God's Word and truth. The battlefield truly does begin in the mind. Stop the onslaught from the Enemy before it reaches the heart.

We will be far from perfect with our rejoicing. We have suffered with addictions and suffered our lives with sin. We have longed for a quick and immediate fix to the problems we could not overcome. God has given us forgiveness and enabled us to feel some joy and peace. We are still human, however, and will at times fight ourselves. We must not give up, give in, or give out along this journey. Remember, God will correct us. We will long for complete healing immediately, but some healing takes longer and has a greater purpose for God's glory when accomplished.

"He has made everything beautiful in its time. Also He has put eternity in their hearts, except that no one can find out the work that God does from beginning to end" (Ecclesiastes 3:11).

In Ecclesiastes 3:11, the word "eternity" shouts out at us. That is the difference between our new lives now and the lives to which we once were in bondage. When we surrender to God, repent, and seek to live by His love and guidance, then we sense the birth of eternity in our hearts. This birth comes from God's Spirit and is truth and grace. We can now rest assured upon our eternity. Our eternity will be filled with paradise and God's presence in heaven. Our glorious eternity is reason to rejoice and do good for our Lord and others in this short-term life. Our immediate circumstances carry less weight of urgency when we surrender to our eternal promise.

God loves us. He wants us joyful and doing good in our lives. We can do this if we stay surrendered. There were times in my early walk with the Lord that I did not feel like rejoicing in the least bit. I wanted to slip back into my chamber of despair and self-pity. God gave me the wisdom to identify this for what it was: my selfishness and doubts and my concerns about me and not my focus on others. God gave me the strength at times to thank Him, rejoice, and be hopeful, even when that was not at all my mood. Through this attitude, a pattern is established that will make it harder and harder to return to our old way of thinking. We may suffer at times during this stage of our transformation. God doesn't say this is easy, but He does say His grace is sufficient. Rejoice in the Lord always and give thanks for His blessings. Praise God with all your soul and long to feel more and more of His presence. Pray and talk with God constantly and give no open door for the Devil to enter.

We have spent our entire lives trying to live it our way. How did that work? Give an open mind and heart to God and truly take the words from Ecclesiastes 3:12 to heart. Serve others, rejoice in God's love, and let things fall into place. In time, this will shine light on the real issues that caused us to stray from our God to begin with.

God Knows What Is Best

How do you plan to defend your mind against negative thoughts and pessimism?

_____

_____

_____

_____

_____

_____

_____

_____

_____

_____

_____

_____

_____

Look at the following verses and their emphasis on rejoicing. How can you make it a daily habit to rejoice and have a grateful, kind heart toward God and others?

Deuteronomy 12:7; Psalm 5:11; Psalm 32:11; Psalm 33:21; Psalm 40:16; Psalm 96:1; Isaiah 29:19; Luke 1:47; Acts 16:34; Romans 12:12; Romans 15:13; Philippians 4:4; 1 Thessalonians 5:16

_____

_____

_____

_____

_____

_____

_____

_____

_____

_____

_____

_____

_____

_____

Chapter 3

The World Leads to Death

As for my people, children are their oppressors, and women rule over them. O My people! Those who lead you cause you to err, and destroy the way of your paths.—Isaiah 3:12

After some time of praising God and doing good with our lives—at least as good as we can—we start to feel conviction against the way we lived before. It becomes more and more apparent that our lives were based on the perceptions of our minds and how it was supposed to be, rather than on God's Word. We can see we pursued happiness in all the wrong places and through all the wrong methods. We chased after our dreams and goals that usually amounted to selfish desires and wants. We were truly blinded, but now begin to see—to see clearly for the first time in our lives! We were lost, but now, through God's mercy, we are found. What we usually will identify at this time is just how wrong and misled we have been.

That is exactly what God is telling us in Isaiah 3:12. He points out where our lives, which led us to complete destruction, began. Somewhere along the way, we fell victim to identity theft in this world. We lost our true identities as children of God and became gods in our own minds. Even those of us who felt inadequate and worthless are guilty of a perception of our own divinity. There are a few different ways of accomplishing the same dreadful results of identity theft. We would have to be nearly perfect to escape this snare, to which so many of us fall victim and as a result become in bondage to our own self-shackled chains. I will use myself as an example of this thievery that steers so many astray from their true course in life. I was a fairly good child growing up. I had a normal childhood and was a member of a comfortable middle-class family. My mother watched over her children very closely, and my father was a hardworking man. Sure, they had some arguments at times, but there was a definite sense of security in our home. I looked upon my father as no mere mortal. He was tall, strong, wise, and always seemed in control of every situation in which life placed him. If ever I did wrong and tried to pull the wool over my father's eyes, he knew it immediately. Somewhere along the way, at an early age and to the best of my recollection, I began to feel I could never be the man my father was. There was no good excuse for this. My father never belittled me or made me feel anything other than supported. Sure, he was disappointed in me a few times, but I never felt as if his love for me was any less. Where did such a notion come from in my mind? While my father was alive, he was my best friend and biggest fan, and I knew this. Something made me feel inadequate.

My mother was another example of this. She would fight to death for any one of her children at the drop of a hat. She was a wonderful mother and always put her children first. Make no mistake; she let me know when she was displeased, but never did I feel anything less than loved by my mother. Then I began to notice my attitude around other kids my age and people in general. I never felt like I was on quite the same level. I always saw others as people who had it all together and were perfect. I was like a fish out of water around a crowd and very uncomfortable when I believed the spotlight was on me. In sports, I was a nervous wreck and suffered self-inflicted anxiety before competitions. My biggest fear was that I would lose the game for the team, and they would discover just how big an underachiever I really was. I ended up getting a scholarship in football, and I remember how much I dreaded the thought of my misery continuing another four years. Now, I thought the whole town in which I grew up was watching to see me fall, and if I did, then the truth would finally be out: I wasn't any good to begin with. My drinking took care of the scholarship. I was flunking out and in trouble shortly into the first year and therefore left with my tail tucked between my legs. Freedom at last—but some freedom that was. At the time, it truly did feel like freedom. Some of the pressure and expectations I had mounted upon my shoulders was relieved at the time.

I lost my true identity early on when I began setting expectations for myself and not heeding what God had planned for me. I placed what I felt was a powerful, successful man in front of anything God had to say on the issue. I strived to control and fix any and all circumstances. I was trying to keep the perception going that I had it all together and needed no help. I never dreamed of asking for help—what an embarrassment that would have been! I made myself out to be the complete and total power in my world and in others' world. I tried to manage and conquer all things alone and never cried uncle. I placed myself in the position that God was supposed to have, and I did not have a clue I had done it. After all, any man worth his salt can handle any and all crises on his own, right?

We are part of a society that tells us to make this much money per year to be successful. We are told to drive this kind of car; after all, you don't want the neighbor having one before you. Wear these designer clothes, buy this type of food, give this answer to your critics, etc. The list goes on and on. We are pressured at early ages from peers and society to engage in sex, alcohol, drugs, and rebellious behavior, just to be recognized as cool. The thought of being deemed a Goody Two-shoes or choir boy in today's culture is absolutely terrifying and sure to cause excommunication from the "in crowd." Adults suffer from the same anxiety of unpopularity as our youth do. We trample our brothers and sisters under our feet in order to fill our lustful greed, pride, and selfishness. Coworkers often plot and scheme how to ruin the reputation of those around them in order to rise up above the competition. We idolize self-absorbed sport icons by mimicking their actions and glorifying their accomplishments. We feel we are good parents if we buy our children the most expensive pair of shoes or put on the biggest birthday party in town for them. Too often, our money and possessions take the place of advice and conversation from which our children really could benefit. We roll red carpets out for movie stars who have a different husband or wife every eighteen months—and those are the devoted ones. We watch television programs that display one example after another of no morals or values and demeaning images that stick like glue in our minds. Too often, pornography has set the expectation of what love and sex is meant to look like. Adults and children suffer from the same deceitful lie that somehow the filth we see is representative of how our intimate relationships should appear.

We place all our resources, time, and abilities into pursuing what the world tells us is important. Material things and ball games on Sunday have surpassed the Bible and church. We set ourselves as prisoners in our own minds of greed and selfishness. We not only feel the need to keep up with society, a lot of us feel we have to be the overwhelming conquerors of society to reach happiness. We chase the American dream, but maybe the dream isn't worth chasing any longer. If the dreams and pleasures of this world lead us into the damnation of our eternal souls, what good are they? If these current expectations and highways to success are burdened with depression and criticism, are they truly holding the key to happiness? The world will have us chasing our identity—or should I say, what we think our current identity in the world needs to be—every single minute of the day. It is easy to get lost and become completely hopeless on the path on which the world guides us. It is a broad, wide path that leads to death!

You have heard me mention the Enemy a few times in previous chapters. Let me bring him into the conversation again. Satan, the Enemy, pretty well runs things down here on earth. Satan was cast out of heaven for the following reasons: pride, ego, selfishness, and greed. He wanted to be like God and above God Himself. Sound familiar? The majority of the world suffers from these same issues. At times, they may manifest in other forms. These are harder to identify but feed off the same principles—fear, doubt, worthlessness, and despair. How do these very different problems relate? Fear can be the same as pride in opposite fashion. When we are fearful, we say we do not want to be exposed or revealed, as opposed to being the main object of attention.

There may be something I don't like about myself or others may exploit. Doubt is a lack of ego and longing for more. Worthlessness is a feeling opposite of selfishness—or is it? We say we're not good enough and don't deserve anything but groan for attention and comfort. We actually are saying to everyone who listens, "Please focus on my feeling better!" Finally, despair is feeling like we have less and less of what we need and long for. That is a disguised version of greed. Satan will get to know us and realize if we are strong or weak in all these areas. Then, he will fuel the fire once he sees an imbalance that can be used to destroy the human most soundly. Sometimes he will fuel several different fires within us at once, making us completely in bondage to the world and hopeless. He will not give us a chance to catch our breath. The flames will consume us and burn 'til all remnants of God are disposed of from within the human heart.

The world truly does lead to death. We will not overcome it by our own resources. We need to look at who we were and from what God has delivered us. We humans alone cannot overcome Satan when we are subjected to the world and give in to its identity theft. The one and only hope is in God. When we realize our past mistakes and just how wicked and deceitful the world and our Enemy can be, we should give praise and thanks to our Father, each and every day, for delivering us from the past. God has taken us off the broad path and set us on a new journey where the path is narrow and straight … straight to His kingdom! During this process we will see many things about ourselves of which we will not approve. Remember, God has forgiven us and loves us. Do not get caught up in guilt and shame of which our heavenly Father has set us free. Satan will be lying in wait to penetrate any crack in the fortress of God upon which we are building within our minds and souls. Rejoice and do good! Infection cannot set in the body that has the remedy in its veins. God's Word is the remedy.

The World Leads to Death

Have your views of success in this world changed?

_____

_____

_____

_____

_____

_____

_____

_____

_____

_____

_____

_____

_____

_____

Look at the following Scripture verses and relate how they speak of the sinful life of the world to which we can fall victim. Also, notice how we are told we have been delivered from this world, and share how the verses speak to you: John 17:13–26; Romans 1:16–32; Romans 12:2; Ephesians 4; Titus 3:3–5.

_____

_____

_____

_____

_____

_____

_____

_____

_____

_____

_____

_____

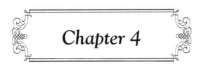

Chapter 4

Surrender Your Trust and Peace to God

Surrender to God's Will and Holy Spirit

> Then the Spirit lifted me up, and I heard behind
> me a great thunderous voice: Blessed is the glory
> of the Lord from His place!—Ezekiel 3:12

All the chapters to this point have placed the emphasis on surrender. We have two more verses to look at in the phase of surrender, as formatted in "3:12 Transformation Ministries". This particular chapter and verse is the one that truly enabled any chains of bondage that remained to shatter with an understanding of truth never before felt in my soul. In the section of chapter 1 called "God Loves Us" (Proverbs 3:12), I spoke of a revelation when I first felt and believed God's love for me. I will explain in this chapter another revelation that completely altered my direction in life and placed my journey in the hands of the Lord.

I had begun seeking counseling and guidance from Pastor Tom Zobrist at Liberty Bible Church in Eureka, Illinois. Although this was a local church, within twenty miles from where I had lived all my life, it was far from any previous church atmosphere I had ever known. People seemed happy to be there and not at all rushed to get to their cars as soon as the service ended. It was as if they enjoyed themselves and enjoyed each other's company. I had been used to attending church where people did not communicate with each other outside a simple hello, good-bye, or "how's work?" Also, I always felt like the entire church was staring at me in judgment of my past or present distress with alcoholism or my marriage. But this church felt different. I felt welcomed and accepted. I remember thinking, *This is odd. These people act as if they like the fact that I am here and not like I am offending them by showing my face in chu*rch. I tried to convince Teresa to attend with me, but at the time, she still was not quite sold on my newfound optimism. She was not sold on me at the time either, to be perfectly honest.

Pastor Tom met with each of us individually and asked our history—events that brought us where we were and where we wished to go from that point. He suggested marriage counseling and spending as much time with fellow Christians as possible. As I've mentioned, Teresa was not sold on all that just yet. I, however, being the reason again for any hardships between Teresa and me, was very cooperative and eager to take Tom's advice. I began meeting with him once per week, attending church to hear him every Sunday, and fellowshipping with a few of the church members who gave wonderful support and encouragement to me when I needed it most. Pastor Tom recommended I undergo a new-believer's study course with him. I have to admit, I felt a little above the new-believers stuff. After all, I had been raised in a church most of my life. I had performed all the required sacraments and requirements and believed in God and Jesus. But I figured God had a reason for the course, and if I truly desired to change my life, it was best to be open-minded and willing.

I studied the booklet he gave me for the course, filled out the questions at the end of each weekly assignment, and discussed the assignment with him each week when we met. This gave me more and more opportunity to read, study, research the Bible, and dive deeper into topics of faith into which I had not looked before. I knew a lot of the Bible stories from childhood and many names of the stories, but at this time, I began to see the readings meant much more. The Bible was speaking directly to me, my circumstances, and my feelings. It was every bit as relevant to me in this day and age as it was when it was written a few thousand years ago.

I was feeling optimistic and encouraged by the direction my life was heading. I had moved past blaming myself, surroundings, God, and others for every negative memory of the past, with honest accountability and remorse for my actions. I no longer wished for death or questioned why I had ever been born. I felt the love, forgiveness, and presence of God for the first time in my life. I was learning, through God's Word and other Christians, to rejoice and do good deeds for others. I looked at my past wickedness and doubts, fears and failures, disappointments, and betrayals, and I honestly recognized the error of my selfish ways. What was missing? Why had I not stumbled on to this new life in God long before now? Why was I unable to control my recovery and surrender up to that point? This is exactly the question I asked Pastor Tom one afternoon: "Why could I not come to this understanding and surrender before, Pastor? Why did I try so hard to control things, with the best of intentions at the start, only to fail time and time again?"

Then Pastor Tom responded with a simple but profound statement I will never forget: "If you could have overcome these things on your own, why did Jesus Christ hang upon the cross?"

I only can explain with words that will not do justice to the feeling I had at that moment. My eyes were opened! My ears finally, truly heard! I understood! I sensed a feeling of warmth and tingles run through my body. I felt a release of weight and a surrender of questions. I felt an approval from the Lord our God, as if He was saying, "You finally hear the truth I have tried to show you!" Whatever weight of shame, guilt, and despair was still hanging upon me was dropped at that very instant. Oh, how I had missed who Jesus Christ was and what He had done! My eyes were filled with tears of joy and acceptance of forgiveness and salvation. Jesus truly had paid my penalty. That is why He hung on the cross. Christ knew I would fall short of the glory of God. Christ knew I would battle the world and the lusts contained in it and on my own power would lose the battle in epic proportion. Jesus took the beatings so I could be forgiven of my wrongs. Christ took the scourging so I could avoid punishment of hell. Jesus was crucified and died upon the cross to give me a hope of life. Our Lord, Jesus Christ, rose from the dead to give me victory over sin and the death I knew in this world and provide everlasting life with the Father in heaven. Jesus did this for me! Jesus did this for all of us! I never saw Jesus Christ as my one and only personal Savior before that day. Then I remembered that the Father and the Son are one and realized that Jesus Christ, my God, died for us because of the great, unquenchable love He has for us all. How much He must love us!

I left the meeting that day with a new outlook on everything in life. Forgiveness of oneself and belief in forgiveness from our God is an overwhelming emotion of hope and power that turns into faith and peace. I truly experienced peace—peace that I had never known or thought possible. How can the brutal death of a man who was nailed to a cross, ridiculed, and scorned give a person such peace? Through His sacrifice of love, He gave His life as ransom for all our sins. All we have done against God that we could never make right by our own works is erased the instant we accept Jesus Christ's sacrifice for us and ask Him into our hearts. This is the moment when we hear the truth and accept it for what I believe truth is: God's grace!

"Because of the hope which is laid up for you in heaven, of which you heard before in the word of the truth of the gospel, which has come to you, as it has also in all the world, and is bringing forth fruit, as it is also among you since the day you heard and knew the grace of God in truth" (Colossians 1:5–6).

The deepest fear of our souls is what happens after death. Jesus Christ removes that fear when we ask Him into our hearts and seek His example in our everyday lives. The fear turns into faith of who we are and where we are going. We are children of God, beloved and precious; we are children who will spend eternity with their loving Father in heaven. Regardless of our past, Christ gives us forgiveness and a future. My spirit was filled with newfound hope, optimism, conviction, and longing to follow the example Jesus set for us. God's Holy Spirit lifted me up to a new height and gave me understanding and insight on His power, glory, and love through Jesus Christ. I even remember feeling lighter when I walked out of the church that day. God gave me a surge of faith that has stayed upon me and increased over time. True worship and praise flowed from my lips more readily, and the awesomeness of God was true to me as never before.

The burden I felt removed was a releasing from the guilt of which I previously could never let go. How could I have? I believed by my own power I could eventually make things right, be the man I was supposed to be, and overcome alcoholism and the world. I failed every time and always made issues worse and more desperate. The burden of guilt and failure grew heavier with each failed attempt. Jesus Christ hung each of our bags of burdens upon the cross in the form of His flesh. Why should any of us carry the burden any longer that Christ took away from us? If we choose not to accept Christ's sacrifice, as we have done so many times before, we are telling God, "Thanks for the thought, but no thanks." If we once again take the selfish attitude that we can handle things on our own and keep God at a safe arm's length away, we are removing our burdens from the cross and carrying them again. Jesus Christ died for this freedom that we can share and feel. Why should we mock any longer the ultimate sacrifice He made for us and threaten our eternity, separated from Him? As humans, we cannot imagine God's wisdom and sovereign power. In this wisdom, He chose the sacrifice of His Son as our atonement for sin. I plead with you all to make the decision in your hearts to accept this sacrifice presented to us from God, our Father Himself, and cease your disbelief in the cross of Christ. Through the cross we are set free, and all things in time will be revealed to us.

God's power is awesome and great! God's mercies and forgiveness are bountiful and abundant. God's love is greater than all! We all will have different testimonies of true surrender. I am blessed to share mine with you. I do want to express that through this stage of surrender and transformation, we are further prepared for God's will for each one of us individually. We are increasingly accessible for God's Holy Spirit to fill us. As we see in Ezekiel 3:12, there will come a time during our surrender when God will lift us up to a higher level of truth and spiritual awareness. Our stories will differ, but I believe we all will have a distinct personal experience during our surrender—at the moment we realize God's Holy Spirit is lifting us up and taking us where we could never go alone. God's Spirit will supply our surrender if we follow in faith. We are asked to supply willing hearts. Our paths and purposes become clearer and will be pointed in one main direction and toward one man in particular. Jesus Christ is the way, the truth, and the life.

Humility and Peace: Trust in the Lord

I will leave in your midst a meek and humble people and
they shall trust in the name of the Lord. —Zephaniah 3:12

Surrender! The same word I heard all my life; the same word I
frequently tried to master by my own will so many times. The word
itself is just a series of letters formed into a three-syllable sound that
explains an event in one's life or a decision of one's life. But I realized
surrender was so much more than a word or temporary decision.
Surrender was an action that, if truly brought forth from sincerity,
would control my journey for the remainder of my life. This action
required a releasing of things that I'd never felt necessary before—
letting go of things I once believed were positive traits but were
negative attributes disguised as values. I'd been completely wrong
on my viewpoint of surrender in previous years. I'd felt my surrender
would relate to a happy family and an ability to control things
without causing damage. I believed it would supply wisdom and
peace in this world from my own resources and accomplishments.
That was surrender to me—the ability to avoid a future failure
because of my willpower to control the events in my life.

I felt the issues that needed to be surrendered in earlier years
were alcohol and my weak willpower. If I could get past those two
glaring downfalls, all else would fall into place, and life would be
smooth. I really believed I could strengthen my willpower, as if
building muscles of the body, by my own means. What a fool I was!
Surrender was not at all what my perception had made it out to
be. I remember feeling this shortly after accepting Jesus Christ as
my personal Savior and Lord, but the funny thing was, I was not
ashamed of the fact that I had been wrong for so many years. To be
honest, I was relieved. I knew from that moment on that my failures
and disappointments and the ability to fix them were beyond my

control or anyone else's without Jesus Christ. Therefore, a new form of surrender took place in my life.

What truly needed surrendering that had not been in previous years? What truly needed embracing that had been neglected in prior attempts? We must surrender our resentment toward others and our resentment toward ourselves. We must let go of our past shame and guilt. We must cast aside our previous forms of healing and become open to the healing of God. We must surrender the false identity the world has implanted into our minds for as long as we can remember. Do not fall again into continued dwelling on the past, and look ahead in hope of the goodness and promises to come. We must surrender our selfishness and attempts to control our very surrender. We have failed and will fail by our own power!

Surrender your every ounce of being to Jesus Christ and His teachings. Jesus surrendered all for each one of us. He set the example of surrender. Give willingly and openly of yourself. Be a servant and a kind soul to all those you know, whether they are family, friends, or strangers. Be obedient to God's Word and will for you, even if led to death, in order to accomplish that will. If we are truly honest, then we see that is where our surrender in Christ leads us—death to the selfish world we have known; death from sin, death from wickedness, and new life in God through Jesus Christ.

During this transformation, we are given the faith and strength to identify, confess, and embrace this wisdom God is showing us. I began to look at myself through very different eyes than I had before. I had a sense of humility I'd never before experienced—not humility in the sense of shame in any means. I humbly confessed my failures and sins in front of my fellow brothers and sisters, with the confidence I was forgiven by God for all of them. I was humbled at the fact God loved me to the point of condemning His Son to death that I may have salvation. I knew my place; I was not an all-powerful human who needed to prove to everyone that no matter what I had been through, I was still standing, due to my special abilities to fix things. I was simply a man who was shown grace and love through God, our Father. I was given forgiveness for my transgressions because of Jesus Christ alone. Nothing I had done was responsible for my transformation. All I had done was ask God for forgiveness and accept Jesus Christ into my heart. My only part to play was true surrender; as true as humanly possible. I need to surrender each and every day to my Lord, and that will never change. Unfortunately, at times my surrender is still too late, and I say things I regret, but they are quickly identified and resolved with humility and ownership. I am not perfect, and neither will you ever be. I do trust, however, that continued growth in Christ will bring us closer and closer to perfection and eternity with our Father in heaven.

Surrender! Surrender is trust and willingness to be led, taught, provided for and, if need be, corrected by beliefs in our lives. That is what surrender means to me today. Zephaniah 3:12 tells us that God will leave in the midst of His people meekness, humility, and trust in the name of the Lord. I made a choice that I press toward each and every day to surrender my life to God and His Son, Jesus Christ. I fall short some days, and you will too. But surrender is a lifelong process, not an overnight process. For our lifelong journey, there are certain things we need to do. Study the Word of God. Fill our minds with Jesus Christ's example of surrender, again and again. Place our time and resources in trusting God and His plan for us. Become a servant and a blessing to others. Our prayer life needs constant attention. We need to let God hear from us as much as possible and be open to hear from Him. We must stay surrendered and realize that Jesus Christ died on the cross to forgive us of our sins, relieve us of past hurts, and bestow within us happiness, joy, and hope of a new life in Him. I am willing to follow the Man who loved me to the point of giving His life for my well-being. I am willing to lay all my prayers and dreams before the throne of God and ask for His guidance and wisdom. If God spared not His Son for us, why would He spare His guidance and wisdom if we ask? Trust in the Lord our God, and stay humble in His presence and thankful in His ears.

At times, we will want to pull back our surrender for our own defense, righteousness, and selfishness. I would wager that Jesus wanted to avoid the cross and the anguish as a human and not bear the humility it caused Him to suffer. What gave Him the ability to stay surrendered to God's will? I believe it could have been only His undying faith and trust in the Father. What an example Jesus set for us! He had the ability to crush the crowds of people and all involved with His wrongful persecution, yet He followed the will of the Father and remained surrendered. Christ remained meek, humble, and obedient in the Father. To me, meekness often meant weakness before my new life in Christ. The actual definition of meekness in biblical terms is very different:

Meekness is an attitude of humble, submissive, expectant trust in God and a loving, patient, and gentle attitude toward others. Meekness is also the restraint of great authority and power with obedience on when to exercise that authority.

Meekness withstood the cross. Humility and trust remained obedient to God the Father. Expectant hope and faith made it possible for Jesus to surrender His will to the Father's will. Meekness is power to subdue our fears and selfishness for the betterment of all around us.

Our Savior not only gave us eternal salvation and life but the greatest example of trust and humility from which we could ever learn.

Surrender to God's Will and Holy Spirit

Do you believe God's Holy Spirit will guide and strengthen you? Do you have an experience where you believe this happened?

_____

_____

_____

_____

_____

_____

_____

_____

_____

_____

Look at the following Scripture verses and share how they identify God's Holy Spirit's providing what is needed and empowering us through life: Ezekiel 36:27; Zechariah 4:6; John 4:24; Romans 8:11, 15; 1 Corinthians 3:16; 2 Timothy 1:14.

_____

_____

_____

_____

_____

_____

_____

_____

_____

_____

Humility and Peace: Trust in the Lord

Explain what you believe God is asking of us when surrendering to Him as Jesus surrendered to Him.

_____

_____

_____

_____

_____

_____

_____

_____

_____

_____

Look at the following Scripture verses and relate the importance we are to see by being humble, meek, and trusting in the Lord: Numbers 12:3–7; Psalm 25:9; Psalm 37:11; Zephaniah 2:3; Matthew 5:5; Matthew 11:28–30; James 4:6.

_____

_____

_____

_____

_____

_____

_____

_____

_____

_____

Believe

Chapter 5

Believe in God's Mercy and Guidance

God Is Merciful

> Go and proclaim these words toward the north, and say:
> Return, backsliding Israel, says the Lord; I will not cause
> My anger to fall on you. For I am merciful, says the Lord;
> I will not remain angry forever.—Jeremiah 3:12

We have reached the point of surrender—true surrender for the first time in our lives. A few questions at this time: will we stay surrendered to something in which we cannot believe? Will we stay surrendered to something we believe will not have mercy upon us? Will we stay surrendered to something that will remain angry with us forever? We might for a while, but it will not last. God tells us to believe His anger will not last forever and that He will be merciful. He does stress that we need to be responsible for our sins and confess them. He tells us to return to Him and acknowledge with a broken and contrite heart that we turned away from Him to begin with (Jeremiah 3:13). We may have some legal responsibilities or relational consequences through our sinful life with which we need to deal, but we must believe God is satisfied with a repenting heart and will lead us in His loving care. Our requirement is to take the responsibility for our previous actions.

King David speaks these words of God in the Psalms:

"The sacrifices of God are a broken spirit, a broken and contrite heart-these, O God, You will not despise" (Psalm 51:17).

God's Spirit will guide us along the way and supply peace and confidence that we never knew when coping with our penalties to society, employers, or loved ones. It really falls back to Proverbs 3:12 at this point. God does love us and will correct us! We may have some situations left to deal with, but if we are truly surrendered to God, He will lessen many of the consequences for us. God is powerful, divine, and all-knowing. We must not return to a pity party at this point in our transformation due to circumstances we have brought upon ourselves. We truly must believe it is all part of God's correction for us. God has promised us an open door through which we can return. If we lose sight and hope of the hallway of God's grace for us, the one that extends beyond our entry door, we could step out from His doorway of mercy, through our own disbelief, and jeopardize our surrender. Believe that you will be a recipient of mercy, grace, and above all, God's love!

How many times have you surrendered to someone who kept throwing all your past mistakes in your face each time you showed the slightest sign of trouble? You might have seen employers go into defense mode as soon as any perceptions of repeated circumstances arise. How often have you been stereotyped by the world as a horrible spouse, awful child, terrible person, and all-around loser, regardless of your best efforts to do things right and with no evidence you have faltered in any way?

Surrender usually constitutes a time of having to work our way out of the doghouse and regain confidence in others' eyes. With God, we are out of the doghouse immediately, once we offer Him our earnest request of forgiveness and repentance. God wants us to believe now that we are forgiven, and He will be merciful to us, currently and in days to come. There is no need to regain God's love and mercy. It has always been there and always will be.

"So when Jesus had received the sour wine, He said, 'It is finished!' And bowing His head, He gave up His Spirit" (John19:30).

These were the final words spoken by Jesus during His crucifixion and death upon the cross, as recorded in the gospel of John. "It is finished!" Why were these words chosen by God to be the last ones we would hear from the mortal life of Jesus Christ? There could have been a final commandment or perhaps a final promise of things to come; maybe a final word of knowledge to His followers, or an encouraging gesture of new life that would again arise.

I believe the Lord spoke all these things to us through those three beautiful words, "It is finished!" Jesus was commanding us to believe that through our faith in His sacrifice and repentance of our sins, the reign of sin directing our souls was finished. There was a promise that the season of oppression and burdens weighing upon our hearts was finished through the grace and love supplied by acceptance of His death as our atonement to God. Knowledge comes to those who hear the words of God with faith and belief, bringing forth a finish to the ears that have been deaf to the good news of the gospel and ushering in new hope to the followers of Christ. And finally, the power of death over our mortal lives lost its hold; it was finished as soon as our spirits confirmed God's eternity through the resurrection of new life through Christ; with belief, we also are reborn anew! Let go of the past and all its doubts, which will destroy the future. We must believe it is truly finished. Our former lives and identities have been left at the cross. That season, if we are seeking God's direction and guidance, is finished!

In Jeremiah 3:14–15, God again tells us to return to Him. He calls us His children, to whom He is married, and He will lead us back to Zion (eastern hill of Jerusalem, where Jesus and His followers will stand in triumph on His second coming; Rev.14:1). God tells us He will give us shepherds according to His heart, which will mentor, lead, and guide us along our transformations. God also says He is married to us within these verses. God is faithful, true, loving, and loyal. He will not be the adulterous husband that I once was. He has made a covenant with us and will not break His word. In ministry, I have come across several men and women who claim they once walked with God but fell away from Him. Their question is always the same: "I have backslid so far. Can God truly forgive me again? Can I feel His presence again?" My response to them is also always the same: "God has answered that question. Ask God if He forgives you. Tell Him you have walked away, and you wish to come back home to Him. Read Jeremiah 3:12–15, and tell me what God says to you."

Time and time again throughout the Bible, God tells us of His mercy and forgiveness. Even when we have knowingly walked away from God so many times, He still will take us back and claim us as His children. We cannot go any further in our transformation with God until we truly believe we receive that forgiveness and mercy. Satan does not want us to believe in the liberty and freedom God has given us. Satan prefers to see us doubtful and remorseful, imprisoned within our minds, and nowhere close to feeling liberated and free. We cannot progress with God if we do not believe in His forgiveness. We must embrace and trust in this truth.

Once you have surrendered to the best of your ability, belief must start planting deep roots of faithfulness within your heart and spirit. Surrender is not possible without beginning with some sense of faith and belief. Faith and belief will not grow without willingness to remain surrendered and trusting. Surrender and belief must be one union, a marriage together, strengthening and encouraging each other to become all they are meant to be, individually and together. They must accompany one another and walk hand in hand through our transformation and the lives we will live. God gives us the 3:12 Transformation with the message that we must anchor our beliefs and surrender upon His words, and portray those beliefs through our lives. God has given us the grace and truth to truly surrender to Him. He has supplied us with the faith needed to believe in His love and mercy. This great work that God is performing in our lives must be resolved and spiritually in agreement. And what God has brought together, let no man separate—including you!

God will not do what the rest of the world will do. God merely asks for your return to Him and confession of how you left Him to begin with. His mercy is yours from that point on. Believe you are given that mercy, no matter what life has in store for you currently or in the days to come. You have been reconciled to God through Jesus Christ. If your heart truly has surrendered to God's will, then you will have a new slate. Believe you are forgiven, not merely given a furlough.

God Has the Answer

> Then the tax collectors also came to be baptized, and
> said to him, "Teacher, what shall we do?"—Luke 3:12

John the Baptist was sent before Jesus Christ to pave the way for the kingdom of God. God used John to be His messenger and to point the people in the direction of correction. The direction was repentance and change from within. This verse speaks of tax collectors in the time of John and Jesus. Tax collectors were considered as untrusting, immoral, and lowly people in the Jewish society, not only by their brethren but also by the Romans who occupied the country. These were the people willing to sell out their fellow countrymen for profit, usury, and personal gain. The true meaning of a traitor and dishonest person was exemplified in the tax collectors of that time. Sound anything like the majority of society today? These people were willing to do anything for their personal greed and success, regardless of who they wronged, regardless of their reputation and beliefs. These kinds of people were the worst-viewed citizens in that time. Yet even they came to John through the Word of God, seeking the answers on how to change their lives and be made new with God. They believed in John the Baptist as a man of God and prophet. They believed God spoke through John and the guidance John gave was the only way to be saved. They were willing to listen and do whatever necessary to follow this new life of hope. The guidance John gave was to make ready, repent and be prepared, confess their sins, and be baptized. John also told the people that One was coming whose sandal strap John himself was not worthy to loosen. He would bring forth the true baptism of the Holy Spirit.

John, of course, was speaking of Jesus Christ. John was pouring his heart out to the people of the region to believe that the time of forgiveness of sins through the Messiah and Savior was at hand. John's one purpose was to make people believe their Savior was coming. This is He who hung on the cross for all of us to be saved and transformed—Jesus Christ! God gave the answer through John the Baptist to lead the people to Jesus Christ and believe He was the Savior.

Today's "tax collectors" are a diverse group made up of alcoholics, drug addicts, prostitutes, drug dealers, adulterers, thieves, dishonest politicians, sex offenders, crooked businessmen, sexual immoralists, gangs, etc. This entire group is made up of individuals worried about themselves and what they lustfully desire in life to satisfy their needs and wants. They will do almost anything and trample over almost anyone to attain their objectives. I was one of these tax collectors before knowing Jesus Christ. There are many tax collectors today who will hear and respond to the plea of repentance and ask God, "What must I do?" What must we do to be saved? We all need Jesus Christ! Only through believing in God's Word and repentance in God's name can we attain the instructions of transformation needed to make us new. This is true for each of us, individually and as a people as a whole. Our entire nation needs this call of repentance. We, as a nation, need to seek the words of God with a repenting heart, if America has any hope of retaining mercy from God the Father and becoming new again. We humans can come up with new programs and action plans to rebuild our communities and nation. Some of these may prove successful and positive for a time, but they will not last or bring forth the true change we require. Our change needs to be spiritual. Our individual and our nation's crises are from a lack of God's presence in our lives. God must be our answer and guide to true change and our resolve to issues we cannot overcome through our own power. We must believe that God has the answer, and we must call upon His name with the request, what must we do? Believe, believe, believe, and pray to God to strengthen your belief each and every day. Our transformation from this point on needs to reflect Jesus Christ's teachings and life example He laid out for all of us through ultimate love.

I want to touch on the Baptist part of John the Baptist. At this stage of our transformation, we believe more each day, with growing faith. We experience sustained peace and confidence that God will not turn His back on us. After all, through honesty and repentance, we should have confessed we were always the one who turned our backs on God. I became convicted in my heart to be baptized at this time of my personal transformation. I wanted to proclaim Jesus Christ as my Savior and be held accountable, not only by God but also by other fellow brothers and sisters of the new life in Christ, which I was given and had chosen. Several months later, after becoming part of a church family, I did just that. I went to the Cedar River, not too far from our church, and was baptized in front of the whole congregation. Praise God, Teresa was baptized with me that very day as well. We both had been baptized previously—me at birth, and Teresa after our marriage and her conversion to my denomination. But baptism meant much more. When I was a baby, my parents did the right thing in promising to God that they, as my parents, would raise me according to God's Word and be godly examples for me. What did I have to do with that baptism? I was an infant with very few concerns—eat, sleep, get my diaper changed, stay warm, eat, and eat (I've always been fond of the eating part). I felt drawn to be baptized shortly after accepting Christ into my heart, and that feeling did not leave. I came to understand baptism through the Scriptures and further believe it was a representation of Christ's death and resurrection into new life. I also believed my public baptism was a confession of the belief that through Christ's sacrifice and my repentance, I was dying to the old life of sin I had known and being reborn in new life with Christ—transformed!

We must believe this new life in Christ is a life long journey and decision. Our public baptisms are a way to proclaim our belief and further pleases our Lord. I also believe that through my baptism, I was further opened to God's Holy Spirit and was being prepared to understand the message He was about to show me.

God Is Merciful

In your words, what do you believe God is saying to you in Jeremiah 3:12–15?

_____

_____

_____

_____

_____

_____

_____

_____

_____

_____

Look at the following Scripture verses and relate what they say to you about God's mercy: Exodus 6:6–9; Deuteronomy 7:6–9; 2 Corinthians 5:17; Ephesians 2:4–8; Hebrews 8:12.

_____

_____

_____

_____

_____

_____

_____

_____

_____

_____

God Has the Answer

Do you believe you have heard God's call of repentance? Are you willing to do whatever necessary to answer your call?

_____

_____

_____

_____

_____

_____

_____

_____

_____

_____

Look at the following Scripture verses and share how they relate to God's guidance and answers being the only hope for salvation and correction: Psalm 32:8; Psalm 119:105; Proverbs 3:5–6; Isaiah 30:21; Isaiah 48:17; Hebrews 13:20–21.

_____

_____

_____

_____

_____

_____

_____

_____

_____

_____

Chapter 6

Belief and Faith in Jesus Christ

Believe in Jesus's Teachings

> If I have told you earthly things and you do not believe, how
> will you believe if I tell you heavenly things?—John 3:12

Listen to this verse! Read it again, and truly let who is asking it
sink into your heart. This is Jesus Christ, our Lord and Savior.
In this verse of Scripture, Jesus is speaking with Nicodemus.
Nicodemus was a member of the Pharisees, which was one sect
of the Jewish religious leadership. Jesus is explaining that lest a
man be born again, he can no way enter into the kingdom of God.
Nicodemus asks Jesus, "Can a man enter into his mother's womb
a second time and be born?" Jesus explains the rebirth of a man
through the Spirit. Nicodemus asks, "How can these things be?"
Jesus replies with the verse on which this chapter focuses from
John 3:12. Jesus tells Nicodemus—and all of us—we must believe
that what He is teaching pertains to this life and this world so that
we are able to have faith enough to believe and seek the kingdom
of heaven to come.

Jesus makes it very clear at this point: our surrender to and belief in
God's Word is the determining factor for our success in overcoming

the trials of this world and possessing the faith needed to believe the promises that God has in store for us in the next.

The 3:12 Transformation was birthed upon this very verse from John 3:12. When I awoke at 3:12 a.m. on November 29, 2010, from the dream God had showed me, I felt a presence and communication never before known to me. My eyes were meant to be opened at that time and that moment of my life. I also had the thought, *3:12 recovery*, in an instant, without even realizing what God was about to show me in the Bible. I had no idea the very verse to which He was pointing me was indeed going to further brand that belief and presence I sensed into my spirit. The reading of this Scripture caused me to nearly faint. I remember that night as if it were yesterday and believe I always will. I believed Jesus Himself was giving a direct message to me—His broken sinner to whom He had given mercy, grace, and salvation through the cross. I believed the calling upon my heart was given to me by God, and I believed God wished for this calling to become manifested through His Holy Spirit and my willingness to carry the message. I was willing, I was in awe, and I was in prayer with God, thanking Him for truly revealing Himself to me.

I should explain the "3:12 recovery." After asking my partner, Larry, to join me in this ministry, after much prayer and debate we chose 3:12 Transformation as the only name to call this miraculous gift God has given us. God is transforming us through these Bible verses and His Son. We will be made new, altered from what we knew before. We are being transformed into a new creation!

We kicked around the words recovery, redemption, and transformation. Recovery presented two issues:

1. Recovery is the same person or entity in a repaired state.

2. Recovery is associated with every other get-well group on the planet.

Redemption was a close runner-up for the ministry name, but it resembled fixing and repairing the old man into a redeemed man. Now, I hope I never pass an opportunity at redemption of past mistakes and regrets, but redemption still did not cover the scope of God's plan that Larry and I felt God had in store for us. At this point, we are undergoing far more than recovery and redemption; we are being transformed into a new creation through Jesus Christ. The success and timeline of this transformation is highly dependent upon our beliefs. Jesus is pleading with us to remove our beliefs of the perceptions under which we have lived our lives and follow His teachings. The Gospels are an example and blueprint of how Jesus lived His life and carried out His ministry here on earth. Jesus advises us how to deal with and overcome every situation we will face in life. He also tells us:

"If anyone desires to come after Me, let him deny himself, and take up his cross daily, and follow Me" (Luke 9:23).

Deny ourselves? My life before surrender to Christ was nothing close to denial of myself. I occasionally made a sacrifice for a loved one but almost always with the intent of personal gain. I can honestly say that even when I had the best of intentions in mind, looking back, there was much selfishness involved. After some time as a true follower of Jesus Christ, I began to believe what denial of oneself meant. God shows us time and time again through the Scriptures. As I read the Bible and the Gospels, I began to see Jesus not only performed numerous miracles and the ultimate sacrifice for us, but He also left a blueprint for us to follow. This blueprint is through His teachings and actions. Jesus showed us how to pray, what to ask for, how to worship in spirit, how to defend ourselves against the

Enemy, and above all, to trust in Him and believe He will carry our burdens. Read the Gospels and listen how many times Jesus tells us to have faith; do not be afraid, and believe in Him.

Our lives become so complicated and busy. We get carried away with trying to solve problems, and as a result, we take Jesus out of the picture. We must strengthen our belief through God's Word. Consequently, our faith will continue to grow. When our belief and faith grow, we begin to take our worries and doubts to Jesus Christ at the first sign of unrest, rather than falling into our lifelong routine of trying to control the situation by our own means. This is exactly what Christ is telling us in John 3:12. The apostle Paul speaks it perfectly:

"And do not be conformed to this world, but be transformed by the renewing of your mind, that you may prove what is that good and acceptable and perfect will of God" (Romans 12:2).

How do we renew our minds? We have been given forgiveness and salvation. We have looked at our past and taken responsibility for our wrongs. We have confessed our remorse and repentance to God and asked Jesus into our hearts. We have been freed from the chains of bondage we have known, released from the burden of guilt and shame, and given new hope and peace never before known. Our house is clean for the first time in years. Where do we go from here? In the gospel of Matthew 12:43–45, Jesus tells us of a man whose house has been cleaned and put in order. Unfortunately, the man leaves his house empty and fails to fill it properly. As a result, the man's state eventually becomes worse than ever before. We learn in these verses to fill our clean house that God has provided. Fill it with God's Word. Fill it with prayer and meekness. Fill it with faith and belief that our transformation is underway and will be completed by the promise given to us by God.

If you fail to fill your house, which is your spirit, you will leave plenty of room for the Enemy to move in once again and will fall into the bondage from which you were once delivered. Your situation will be far worse than ever before experienced. I failed to fill my house many times in life, and my fall was greater each time. We can always lower our bottom. Jesus is telling us that it will no longer happen if we believe in Him and His teachings.

On the topic of believing in Jesus, let's look closer at what I believe the confession truly means:

"In the beginning was the Word, and the Word was with God, and the Word was God" (John 1:1).

"And the Word became flesh and dwelt among us, and we beheld His glory, the glory as of the only begotten of the Father, full of grace and truth" (John 1:14).

"He who believes in Him is not condemned; but he who does not believe is condemned already, because he has not believed in the name of the only begotten Son of God" (John 3:18).

In 1:1 and 1:14 of the gospel of John, Jesus was the name given to the Word of God. When we accept Jesus Christ as our Lord and Savior, are we not confessing that we believe and will live as Jesus taught us? Now let's look at John 3:18. When I confess my faith in Jesus, I truly am confessing my belief and obedience to the Word of God. The Word of God is the Bible from cover to cover. We must be obedient to the Word's (Jesus's) teaching throughout the entire Bible. We must believe in the total package, believe in the whole Word, and follow the plan to its entirety the best we can, with guidance from the Word. Too often we like to pick and choose which parts of the Bible we will obey. This is generally based on others' responses or perhaps what our peers believe. We settle for quick gains and comforts, rather than sustained perseverance. Jesus makes things very clear for us in John 3:12: our belief and trust in His way, whether it is the easy way or not, must be resolved. His way is definitely the righteous way that leads to eternal gains and comforts.

My belief exploded off the charts on the morning of November 29, 2010, at 3:12. What I once felt unattainable became reality. God will give each and every one of us the surge of faith needed to strengthen our belief. God's timing is perfect and precise. We merely need to stay surrendered, speak with God as often as we can in prayer, read and study God's Word as much as possible, and remain willing to be taught. One more thing: when you see and hear from God—*believe!*

Faith in Christ

> In whom we have boldness and access with Confidence
> through faith in Him.—Ephesians 3:12

Boldness and confidence—Ephesians 3:12 is explaining how Jesus Christ became the way to manifest God's plan for all of us. Through Jesus we can begin to know the wisdom of God, and His mysteries may be revealed. Jesus becomes our great intercessor to the throne of God Himself. All our prayers and requests are to be given to Jesus Christ, our Lord. We are transforming our lives into true disciples of Christ. We need not take our requests and tribulations to any other source than Jesus Christ and God, our Father.

My faith grows every day along this journey. I pray within my spirit to Jesus, God, and the Holy Spirit as much as I consciously can. I also believe, with seeking hearts, our spirit can be praying to God even when we are unaware of the fact. Jesus truly dwells within our hearts. Romans 8:26 tells us that the Holy Spirit makes intercession for us with groaning that cannot be uttered. Through our faith and belief, we can determine how much of ourselves we give for Christ's dwelling and guidance of the Holy Spirit. Belief and faith are so critical! Our faith will grow the more we read God's Word.

"So then faith comes by hearing, and hearing by the word of God" (Romans 10:17).

"For we walk by faith, not by sight" (2 Corinthians 5:7).

"Now faith is the substance of things hoped for, the evidence of things not seen" (Hebrews 11:1).

"But without faith it is impossible to please Him, for he who comes to God must believe that He is, and that He is a rewarder of those who diligently seek Him" (Hebrews 11:6).

"For by Grace you have been saved through faith, and that not of yourselves; it is the gift of God" (Ephesians 2:8).

These are just a few Scriptures that speak of faith throughout the Bible. But do you see the trend? It's the plea of God to believe! Faith is belief that God will do for us what we could never do. These verses show clearly that our faith and belief grow through God's Word. We then are instructed to walk according to those words, with the belief that they are true and righteous. God tells us to see the hopes and dreams of the end result and believe them. God tells us none of this is possible without the belief and faith required from us to wholeheartedly seek Him. And finally, God reminds us that this was a gift to begin with. We did not earn this salvation; it was granted to us according to some small increment of belief to which we chose to surrender.

Somewhere in our wretched souls, which we possessed before surrender to God, there had to be a small seed of faith that brought us to this point. Just remember, it was a gift. I've often thought surrender was the main part of anyone's recovery and chance at long-term success. Now, I would say that surrender is the biggest part of recovery, but belief is the largest building block along the way of transformation. The transformation God has in store requires a saint-like faith. But that is exactly what each and every one of us is when we surrender our lives to God and ask Jesus into our hearts. God's Holy Spirit will supply the faith needed to believe. Our great intercessor, Jesus Christ, will hear our requests and lay them before the throne of heaven for us. We are not in this battle alone. We never were. If we had been, we would not have the salvation we now know.

At the end of this phase titled "Believe" and speaking of battles from which Christ has delivered us, I think of the battle of Armageddon to come. I realize, at this point of transformation, many have been involved or are involved in their own personal Armageddon. Revelation tells us of the final war, Armageddon.

This war will take place on earth between Jesus and His angels and saints and Satan and the forces of wickedness. But do you ever stop to think of your personal Armageddon (the battle that positions you on the side of Christ to begin with)? Not all Christians will go through the same degree of warfare and battle, but it's safe to say all will encounter this time in their lives when their spirits (through the guidance of the Holy Spirit) becomes involved in spiritual Armageddon, which will anchor their position for the biblical Armageddon to come—the time when our Savior Jesus Christ returns and forever abolishes the evil of this present world. During our personal Armageddon, the Enemy will come at our weaknesses and strengths. This season usually will leave us in the most vulnerable state we could imagine. Any shield of faith we may have had up to this point will be greatly compromised. Rather than being upright and prepared to stop the fiery arrows, our shields will all but fall completely from our grips. We will be as exhausted objects of humanity, on our knees, with what little means of strength remains, merely trying to lift our chins from our chests but petrified to see what lies ahead. Then we will present ourselves as the perfect target for Satan, who will no longer launch fiery arrows but project the nuclear warhead of desolation directly into our souls. We will be truly defeated, bewildered, and longing to cease the tragedy of hopelessness that keeps playing through our minds.

We cannot rely on our own strength and resources. Our best efforts and thoughts will not avail us of anything. We truly will be under the Armageddon of our lives that we will experience upon this earth, the one that will determine which side we will be on for the future Armageddon, which our Lord has revealed to us through His Word. Then, during the midst of this onslaught, we will be reminded of a love that we cannot explain. We will be drawn to a wellspring of perseverance that is not of our resources. We will sense a greater purpose to our lives than the current mourning we are undergoing. We will see shadows of promises made, blessings to come, and victories ahead. We will see all these things and will be made aware of all these emotions through the image of a lamb upon an altar—an altar in the form of a cross.

We will make our allegiance to that Lamb and rely upon Him, regardless of the future we face. We will be given victory over the Enemy! The warhead traveling straight for our souls will be blocked by the altar in the form of the cross, which always was our shield of faith from the beginning. God has chosen us so we, at this particular time of our personal Armageddon, could choose Him.

Choose to serve Him, choose to obey Him, and most of all, choose to fight for Him in the likeness of His Son. We carry this life battle with our fellow brothers and sisters and the personal Armageddons they face. We will carry this fight into the next life as well—to the battle in which we will fight alongside our Savior, when the evils of this world are defeated for good. To God, the Father of our Savior, Jesus Christ, be the glory of all our individual Armageddons and the final one to come.

Continued growth and knowledge in Jesus Christ will lead to more faith and belief. The Holy Spirit will supply peace and understanding never known before. What do you choose to believe in right now? If you are a new Christian embarking on this journey, I ask you to stop and ask yourself that very question. Do you believe that Jesus Christ will hear your requests? Do you believe you are being remade new, transformed, and given a purpose? Do you believe Jesus Christ will see you through to the end? I cannot answer these questions for you. I can answer the question for myself and promise you I believe the answer with all my heart. But I will refer to the Bible, the holy Word of God, for the answer—and you can too.

To sum it up:

"Being confident of this very thing, that He who has begun a good work in you will complete it until the day of Jesus Christ" (Philippians 1:6).

Believe in Jesus's Teachings

What does being a true believer in Jesus Christ mean to you?

_____

_____

_____

_____

_____

_____

_____

_____

_____

_____

Look at the following Scripture verses and relate how they speak to you about being a believer and disciple of Jesus Christ: Matthew 16:24–25; John 6:45; John 14:6; John 15; Philippians 4:9; 1 Peter 4:2; 1 John 2:6.

_____

_____

_____

_____

_____

_____

_____

_____

_____

_____

_____

Faith in Christ

How do you picture yourself becoming bolder and more prayerful in Jesus?

_____
_____
_____
_____
_____
_____
_____
_____
_____
_____

Look at the following Scripture verses and relate the importance of faith and belief: Matthew 9:20–22; Matthew 9:28–29, Mark 11:22–24; Romans 5:1–2; Corinthians 4:13–14; Corinthians 5:6–7.

_____
_____
_____
_____
_____
_____
_____
_____
_____
_____
_____

Live

Chapter 7

God's Individual Plan for Each of Us

Behold, I have done according to your words; see, I
have given you a wise and understanding heart, so that
there has not been anyone like you before you, nor
shall any like you arise after you.—1 Kings 3:12

We have surrendered to God and our belief in Him is growing
stronger day by day. But what is this really leading up to? We are
being transformed into new creations and therefore, a new way
of life and purpose for life will manifest itself. The third phase of
3:12 Transformation is to live—that is exactly what God teaches
us with the verses involved. The "Live" phase contains more
scriptural verses than any other phase of 3:12 Transformation.
The explanation for this is simple: we have lived the majority of our
lives wrongfully seeking and attempting to control our destinies.
Now, we must be spiritually guided to understand God's destiny for
us. We also must be guided daily to learn how to live that destiny
in Christ. We will be shown new ways of thinking, acting, giving,
and understanding. All we have known has been from the human
viewpoint, not from God's viewpoint. We will see God's infinite
wisdom and grace, upon which we will base our new foundation
in Christ. God will reveal this wisdom and direction to us through
His Word and Holy Spirit. God also will show us during this stage

our true uniqueness and individuality and the intimate relationship He desires to have with us.

This is exactly what we see in 1 Kings 3:12. Some background to this verse: King Solomon, king of Israel and builder of the first temple in Jerusalem, has a dream where God speaks to him. God is pleased with Solomon and says to him in the dream, "Ask! What shall I give you?" Solomon thanks God for His mercy, grace, and kindness he has received and the kindness shown his father, King David. Solomon asks for something that, I would venture to say, not too many humans would ask for. Solomon asks God for an understanding heart to judge God's people and discernment between good and evil. In short, he asks God for wisdom, knowledge, and God's presence with him. This request pleases God, and God replies to him with the verse upon which this chapter is based—1 Kings 3:12. In God's reply to Solomon, He not only grants the request, but God also takes it much further and tells him there will never be, nor has there ever been, another king as Solomon. God wants Solomon to understand without a shadow of a doubt that he has an individual calling and relationship with God that no other human can have.

God is telling you that there will never be another Solomon but also, there will never be another you! God gave Solomon his request because it was from a pure, humble, and grateful heart. God also gave Solomon what he did not ask for. He gave him riches and honor that were unmatched by all kings before or after as well. Now, we should not expect to become rich and famous, but we can expect God to show us what our individual calling will be. The calling we receive may be similar to others, but our role for God cannot be fulfilled by any other human. It is our calling and ours alone. It is our commission, and when God reveals it to us, we will know. This is the level of intimacy the Creator of the universe wants to have with the humble, beautiful you!

For You formed my inward parts; You covered me in my mother's womb. I will praise You, for I am fearfully and wonderfully made; Marvelous are Your works, and that my soul knows very well. My frame was not hidden from You, when I was made in secret, and skillfully wrought in the lowest parts of the earth. Your eyes saw my substance, being yet unformed. And in Your book they all were written, the days fashioned for me, when as yet there were none of them. How precious also are Your thoughts to me, O God! How great is the sum of them! If I should count them, they would be more in number than the sand; When I awake, I am still with You. (Psalm 139:13–18)

King David writes of God's great love and affection for him with Psalm 139. David was not privy to this depth of relationship with the Creator alone; this psalm is true for every one of us. We see clearly the intimacy the Lord has with our being. We are formed by God Himself. Creation of life is not an accident; we have a purpose! God has a purpose! God's thoughts toward us are truly wonderful and loving. We are the apple of our heavenly Father's eye.

When we give all we know to give to Jesus Christ, our Lord and Savior, we will be shown how to live. God's Holy Spirit, when sought, will lead us through life on a daily basis. We must seek with a willing and pure heart. It is really no longer about us; it is about living a life set forth by the example of Jesus Christ and striving to please God. All the emphasis on belief leads up to this very stage of transformation. God has freed us. Now it is time to live for Him and take the path in life God will send us on. Be at peace; God Himself will walk along this path with us and fight our battles for us.

"You will not need to fight in this battle. Position yourselves, stand still and see the salvation of the Lord, who is with you, O Judah and

Jerusalem! Do not fear or be dismayed; tomorrow go out against them, for the Lord is with you" (2 Chronicles 20:17).

All that is required is faith and to remain surrendered and let Him fight those battles. Jesus came to give us life and life abundantly. That message is not just for eternal life in heaven but also for the lives we are living today. We did not give ourselves to God merely to live out our days in isolation, mediocrity, and boredom. We give our lives over to God with the hope of better days ahead and dreams of things to come. Jesus Christ died for us to begin experiencing that life of new hope, as soon as we ask Him into our hearts and repent for our sins.

God will prepare in your heart a wise and loving new creation to replace the foolish soul of the world that once occupied His temple. You will be shown how to live by God. You will sense wisdom and discernment through God's Holy Spirit for protection against temptations and snares of the world. Our old lives were filled with sin. Sin leads to death. We are given life. We are given life abundantly! Seek God's intimacy and plans He has for you. Ask Him very clearly in prayer—and not just one time. Humbly ask God daily to show the path for you to follow and that your individual calling is made known through His Spirit. I can witness that God very clearly gave me my own calling. I am following that calling through the ministry of 3:12 Transformation and with this book. I can also witness that I asked for the wisdom and knowledge of what the calling would be for several months leading up to God's revelation. Don't you think King Solomon's request was contained in his heart and prayers long before God ever asked him to give it? Through our honest living for God, we will lose the spontaneous requests for quick satisfaction and let the true desires of our hearts come to light through God's marvelous timing. Do not be discouraged if you do not get your answer as soon as you would like. You may even mistake your calling as the calling of God for a time or two. It's okay. We want to please our heavenly Father, and this may lead to some overzealous reactions at times. Ask yourself this: "if God did not spare His Son and Spirit when I called upon Him during my life of sin and despair, do I think He will not respond now that I am seeking Him as best I can"?

Be patient; you are learning to live all over again. Just believe how much God loves you, and He will make known to you His individual plan for only you. I have one more question to ask you. Do you surrender, believe, and accept living this life and calling that God has for you? If you do *not*, then tell me who can replace you in the eyes of God?

God's Individual Plan for Each of Us

Do you believe God has an individual calling and purpose for your life that only you can perform?

_____

_____

_____

_____

_____

_____

_____

_____

_____

_____

_____

Read all of Psalm 139 and share how you feel it relates to God's intimacy with your existence.

_____

_____

_____

_____

_____

_____

_____

_____

_____

_____

_____

_____

Chapter 8

Laying a Foundation

Build upon the Foundation of Christ

> Now if anyone builds on this foundation with gold,
> silver, precious stones, wood, hay, straw.
> —1 Corinthians 3:12

In the beginning of chapter 1, I spoke on a foundation in Christ. This is the subject we will look at with this chapter—we are God's building.

"For we are God's fellow workers; you are God's field, you are God's building" (1 Corinthians 3:9).

A building for God needs a rock-solid foundation. In the "Live" phase of 3:12 Transformation, our journey depends upon the foundation we build. Stone by stone, we must lay this foundation through our faith and obedience in Jesus Christ and His teachings.

"Behold, I lay in Zion a chief cornerstone, elect, precious, and he who believes on Him will by no means be put to shame" (1 Peter 2:6).

Jesus Christ is our cornerstone. All we do must be anchored upon and adjacent to our cornerstone. We are rebuilding our houses; we are rebuilding our spiritual temples. Our foundation is built upon our obedience to God. If we are to live godly lives through Jesus Christ, we must be founded upon Jesus Christ. Therefore, we must equip ourselves with the proper tools to construct the foundation: faith, kindness, love, hope, good works, perseverance, and selflessness. We must submit our thoughts and actions to Jesus Christ and His teachings to learn and attain these tools.

Our foundations will support the houses we are building. Jesus is not only the cornerstone but also our master builder and outlined blueprint, as we allow ourselves to be constructed through Him. Jesus tells us in Matthew 7:24–27 that a wise man built his house upon a rock. When the floods came and winds blew, the man's house remained. He also tells us that a foolish man built his house on the sand. When the winds blew and the floods came, the man's house could not withstand, and the fall of that house was great. Jesus is telling us to build our foundations and houses upon Him. When we do this, our houses, through Jesus Christ, will stand up against the attacks of the world, the tribulations of life, and the snares of the Enemy. Storms will come, but our houses will remain. If we choose to build our houses upon foundations we have created through the cares of this world, we are choosing to build upon the sand once again. When the winds blow and the floods come through the trials in life, our houses will fall. How can a foundation that is not founded in stone survive? It cannot!

The foundations and houses we build in this life are not merely for this world. Our true foundations will be tested in the life to come on the day we all come before Jesus Christ. First Corinthians 3:12–13 tells us in that day, each one's work will become clear and shall be revealed by fire. The fire will test each one's work of what sort it is. Our works from this moment until that day will be the assembling of our foundations and construction of our houses. There is nothing we can build without Jesus Christ that will withstand the fire. I built a house upon a sand foundation, time and time again throughout my life. I labored upon the foundation with anxiety, fear, resentment, and doubt. Each time when the wind blew and flood waters rose, my house was laid to waste. It truly became a house of desolation. I blindly skipped past the cornerstone that is Jesus Christ in the foundation of every house, leading up to surrender of my life to Christ. I began rebuilding my foundation upon the leftover, washed-out soil, which was the remains of the previous building I had constructed through the world. If Jesus would have returned and the Day of Judgment would have taken place during any of the previous houses I constructed, my house would have been consumed by fire. Nothing would have endured the fire of God. The foundation, if it remained, would have been a bleak example of man's pride and foolishness. Thankfully, God's fire came into my soul before I came before Him on the day of reckoning. God gave me forgiveness and love. God gave me peace and courage. God gave me His Son. Through the Holy Spirit, my soul was consumed by the fire of God, and I was convicted to build one more house. Also, through God's Holy Spirit, I was given humility and wisdom to call upon Jesus Christ to be the foundation of my house and works upon which I would labor.

That is what 1 Corinthians 3:12 tells us. Our foundation in Christ should reflect a life led by Christ. Any and all materials need to come from God's Word. We cannot begin to build a structure that will endure into eternity without an eternal foundation. I want my house supported upon a foundation where my wife will feel secure, my children will feel safe and loved, and my soul will be at peace throughout the storms that will arise. We are given opportunities to strengthen our foundations each and every day through the examples we set in life. Let your example be clearly seen as a follower of Jesus Christ! Build daily upon love, kind acts, and your faith. Pray that your foundation is made strong, and stand up to the fire on the day of the Lord. Our foundations are spiritual.

"I indeed baptize you with water; but One mightier than I is coming, whose sandal strap I am not worthy to loose. He will baptize you with the Holy Spirit and fire" (Luke 3:16).

"For our God is a consuming Fire" (Hebrews12:29).

We see how John the Baptist came to proclaim repentance of sins and baptism in water. The water baptism was symbolic of the person's repentance and the washing away of previous lifestyles that had been led by sin and disobedience of God. John tells us that One is coming who will baptize us with the Holy Spirit and with fire. Fine metals such as gold or silver go through a process where they are subjected to extreme heat. During this process, the metal becomes liquid and separates from any impurities that may be present. These impurities are referred to as slag or dross. The impurities surface, which makes it possible to remove them, and it leaves a more purely refined metal when solidified again. This process must take place many times to attain the purest form of the metal possible. Our God is a consuming fire that is meant to consume the wickedness of sins, the "impurities" from among us. Our faith and discipleship in Jesus Christ will ignite the fire of God within our spirits. This leads to baptism directly by the Spirit of God and can continually purge out the spirit of sin that once controlled the building of our foundations. When we come before the throne of God on our appointed day, a follower of Jesus Christ, who has undergone refinement through the fire of God's Holy Spirit, will be prepared to withstand the refining fire that will test our foundations. Our purest form of God's precious Spirit should be present.

The building of our foundations will go on forever. We must devote the time and obedience to ensure that through Christ, they will endure forever. Now, there will be times when our foundations will be tested. We may see areas of our foundations that have no use for God's kingdom. We are humans still, and on occasion we may try to fit a selfish or fearful stone or two into our walls. God will show us when there is a stone that cannot fit with the foundation He is assembling through us. The foundations we build are for God. Be careful to seek spiritual guidance in performing God's work and not your own. Using myself as an example, if my foundation, ministry, and house are built upon the foundation and will of God, it will stand. If my foundation, ministry, and house are built for my will, all will perish. I believe it is of God and for God. I can assure you, I still have trials and tribulations in life, and you will have your own share also. Do not lose faith. Some days will be glorious and some downright horrible. I am confident the majority will fall in the middle of the two and be filled with peace in knowing God loves us and will guide us. We are laboring upon foundations intended to last forever. We will not complete our foundations overnight.

Continued Growth: We're Not Perfect

Not that I have already attained, or am already perfected;
but I press on, that I may lay hold of that for which Christ
Jesus has also laid hold of me. —Philippians 3:12

God has truly given us an outline of rebirth and transformation to follow. We are building upon our foundations and striving daily to improve, perhaps even aiming to be perfect. Philippians 3:12 tells us to press on and fight the good fight. It also tells us to keep things in perspective. We are not perfect; we are merely broken sinners who have been given grace and mercy through Jesus Christ. Our pursuit toward this perfection in Christ will last the rest of our mortal lives and is only available because of Jesus's making it available to us. We will make beautiful changes by the grace of God as we live this new life in Christ. Be careful not to fall under the illusion that all has been done by your own individual resources and righteousness.

"Fight the good fight of faith, lay hold on eternal life, to which you were also called and have confessed the good confession in the presence of many witnesses" (1 Timothy 6:12).

This is exactly what our continued growth in Christ is all about— eternal life. Through our humble confession of the good news in Christ, we build our faith and plant seeds for God. These seeds, by the grace of God, may one day be used to further enlarge God's kingdom and glory. We are pressing on to lay hold of our eternal lives with Christ by confessing what Christ has done for us. This is done by living a life of faith and seeking further intimacy with God.

You have not been forgiven by your own power, resources, and glory; all you have has come through the One who is perfect—Jesus Christ. You will struggle and at times may regress. You will experience doubt, have moments of lost faith, and have attacks of anxiety and fear. You may believe, for a time, you are not able to complete the journey you have begun—and you will be right; you cannot complete this on your own, but you do not have to do so. You are chosen! You were first convicted and led by the holy, perfect Jesus Christ.

We do not have to be perfect. We only need to press on through the good times and the bad, knowing that Christ will carry us through to the end. We merely need to continue asking to lay hold of Jesus Christ and God's will for us. I am not perfect. As an alcoholic and forgiven sinner, I must look back at the life I led and the way I handled disappointments in the past. I wanted issues resolved immediately. I wanted my pain and suffering removed as quickly as possible. I wanted to be the perfect example of a capable man who could attain resolution by his own resources. I also wanted others to know of my brilliant wisdom and how I fixed all things that had been amiss. I certainly was not perfect but desired to be—I felt any less desire was underachieving. I lived a life of fear, bondage of my thoughts, and futile attempts toward perfection. This book, *3:12 Transformation*, shows a new way to live, through the divine guidance of God. I will no longer live all in for today, although I will give all I have for today. My thoughts of attaining perfection in this life have been replaced with attaining grace for my eternal life. I will give Jesus Christ glory every time I lead a fellow brother or sister to His kingdom and not act as though I am the authority that set them free. Thank God, He does not expect perfection from us as soon as we surrender to His will. If it were a rule that had to be followed to stay in the mercy of God, there would be very, very few people in heaven (if, by chance, you made it there to see).

"For by Grace you have been saved through Faith, and that not of yourselves; it is the gift of God" (Ephesians 2:8).

This new life in Christ is a gift. Jesus hung upon the cross for us when we were all sinners and broken. He will give grace and mercy for us now and also when we fail to be as perfect as we would like to be. Boast not in yourself or your accomplishments. Boast in Jesus Christ and the sacrifice, forgiveness, and victory He has in you!

"For I determined not to know anything among you except Jesus Christ and Him crucified" (1 Corinthians 2:2).

This is our testimony; this is our witness to spread to others. We have been saved. We do not need to be perfect; we only need to further seek the One who saved us and live our lives as an example of His love. Further seek God's wisdom and gifts of the Spirit that He will bestow upon you.

The Devil tries to attack me in this area daily. It is so easy to once again place expectations upon myself that I cannot reach. I judge and criticize my actions. Did I do enough? Did I not do enough? Satan wants me to question my worth and salvation once again. Satan wants you to question the very same thing. Remember, *Satan is a liar!* He tries to twist and pervert the truth. Distractions and misaligned priorities can lead us into false expectations and unachieved results once again. If you give into your accomplishments as the source of your joy, as opposed to God's grace, you can bet you will have a sense of unattainable goals no longer worth striving toward. You should be after consistency—a consistent heart that refuses to let the current situation depict your future outlook. "Pressing" means letting your weight rest upon the source on which you are pressing. As long as you continue to press into God's Word and continue to press into prayer, you will not be supporting your entire weight on your own strength.

Our strength will fail us; God's strength will support us! Discouragement will come at times, but we cannot allow it to dwell in our hearts and take up permanent residency. We must press on in faith to attain the promises that have been given to us by the Lord. Faith delivers an eviction notice to discouragement that reads: "You are no longer permitted to occupy this temple. It is the temple of God"

"Therefore you shall be perfect, just as your Father in heaven is perfect" (Matthew 5:48).

Perfect, in the sense Jesus speaks of it with Matthew (5:48), is the conviction of our souls toward our actions and treatment of others. Jesus instructs us in Matthew 5 to give mercy, forgiveness, graciousness, and love toward those with whom we interact. This can only be accomplished with a pressing-on attitude of God's love and guidance. Our foundations are by no means perfect, but we diligently move ahead in faith to further refine our foundations by extending that love and grace to others, as well as to ourselves.

Different religious denominations have different views on perfection. I will not enter into that discussion in this book. I only want to tell you this: live your life in an attempt to be perfect and holy before the Lord, but do not give up when you realize that may never happen. God will use victories and disappointments to further show you His purpose for your life. You are a work in progress, as you can see in Philippians 3:12. Strive for perfection, even though you'll never get there. But God's Son—He is perfect, and your sin He did bear!

Build upon the Foundation of Christ

In what areas do you see your foundation in Christ as strong? What areas do you feel need to be removed and further refined?

_____

_____

_____

_____

_____

_____

_____

_____

_____

_____

_____

Read Ephesians 2:17–22 and 2 Timothy 2:19–21. What do these Scripture passages say to you about foundations and dwelling places of the Lord?

_____

_____

_____

_____

_____

_____

_____

_____

_____

_____

Continued Growth:
We're Not Perfect

After reading this chapter, share how you plan to continue with hope and faith in your walk with Jesus Christ and not be overcome with discouragement through your own expectations.

_____

_____

_____

_____

_____

_____

_____

_____

_____

Read the following verses and relate how they speak to you on becoming perfect and on true strength: Joshua 1:9; Zechariah 4:6; Psalm 18:32; 2 Corinthians 12:9; Ephesians 3:13–20.

_____

_____

_____

_____

_____

_____

_____

_____

_____

_____

_____

A Tree Is Known by Its Fruits

Become Kind, Meek, and Merciful

> Therefore, as the elect of God, holy and beloved,
> put on tender mercies, kindness, humility,
> meekness, longsuffering.—Colossians 3:12

Living our lives as an elect of God? What exactly does that say to us? Colossians 3:12 tells us that as the elect of God, we are holy and beloved. It tells us to live life mercifully, kindly, humbly, and meekly and with perseverance. The definition of "elect" in this format is those who have heard, believed, and been saved through Jesus Christ and those who have been set apart by the Holy Spirit of God. At this stage of our transformation, if we seek God with true and pure hearts, we should not only believe we are the elect but live in a manner that reinforces this. Our lights should shine brighter for others to see. Let's look at how we lived life before becoming the elect of God and what fruits came forth as a result. My example may relate to many.

Colossians 3:12 says, "Put on tender mercies." Be forgiving toward others. I never allowed myself to forgive those I felt harmed or wronged me. In my mind, I believed I must keep my guard up at all times. Only a fool forgave an enemy. I believed an enemy, more than likely, would cause harm to me again. Then, I would only have myself to blame. Sometimes these people were not even enemies. They might have been family members, coworkers, or children. I believed and lived under the perception that my forgiveness and mercy toward others was a sign of weakness. Forgiveness, I felt, acknowledged I was not perfect and possibly could need forgiveness as well.

What a horrible thought in the mind of a man trying to be God himself. How could the person who hurt me be made to suffer if I forgave him? That person should feel the same pain I felt because of his or her actions. Now, after some mentoring and guidance from God's Holy Spirit, I recognize I was the only person suffering from my unforgiveness. Unforgiveness kept me a captive in strife and resentment—thoughts that occupied my mind as overstaying house guests, refusing to leave.

"For if you forgive men their trespasses, your heavenly Father will also forgive you" (Matthew 6:14).

This verse also says to become kind and humble. Kindness was shown only if I believed people were not a threat to me. If you haven't gathered by now, I pretty well thought everyone was a threat to me. I had moments of kindness but usually only to ensure kindness in return. True kindness, with no expectations of a return upon investment, was seldom performed. I had many cases of being utterly humiliated in life, but no true sense of humility or trust in God existed. In my mind, humility was always something of which I should be ashamed.

"But love your enemies, and do good, and lend, expecting nothing in return; and your reward will be great, and you will be sons of the Most High; for He Himself is kind to ungrateful and evil men" (Luke 6:35).

Likewise, you who are younger, be subject to the elders. Clothe yourselves, all of you, with humility toward one another, for "God opposes the proud but gives grace to the humble" (1 Peter 5:5).

Colossians 3:12 also speaks about meekness and long-suffering. Meekness was weakness, in my way of thinking. I had to be strong and viewed that way by family, friends, and all society. My personal perceptions of meekness were greatly mistaken. Zephaniah 3:12 in chapter 4 speaks of true meekness as I understand it today.

Long-suffering is perseverance, patience, and faith for better days to come; being willing to endure afflictions for the greater purpose and good. Not a common theme to a man such as myself who wanted everything fixed now, immediately, and exactly the way I thought it should be. I hope you see just how blindly and fearfully I lived my life. My fruits reflected my life and the manner in which I lived. Among these fruits were alcoholism, fear, strife, remorse, deceitfulness, lack of self-control, selfishness, shame, and despair.

Our fruits are what abound from us through our actions and way of life. Our fruits are a sign of what our tree is soaking up through its roots. Think of your soul as the tree. The beliefs you have in life, your spiritual foundation, and your values and morals are the roots. From what source do you choose to grow your roots for the nutrients you need to sustain your tree? If your source is the world and the perceptions of success in the world, your fruits probably have a similar taste and appearance as the fruits I brought forth for many years. If your source is Jesus Christ and God's Word and Holy Spirit, expect much different results. Our heavenly Father has told you what these fruits will look like and how others will know you are the elect of God.

"But the fruit of the Spirit is love, joy, peace, longsuffering, kindness, goodness, faithfulness, gentleness, self-control. Against such there is no law. And those who are Christ's have crucified the flesh with its passions and desires" (Galatians 5:22–24).

3:12 Transformation shows us a new way to live, according to God's Word. Jesus Christ set the perfect example for us to follow. Galatians 5:22–24 describes the fruits of the Spirit that will manifest through our transforming lives in Jesus Christ. God's Word will grow from within our hearts and souls and develop a root system that will tap into God's Holy Spirit. True kindness and meekness will be known and demonstrated. True mercy and forgiveness will seem like a possibility and a desire. Humility will be displayed in our ability to trust God and His will for us and our not attempting to be God. We will begin to accept circumstances that are unpleasant, with the faith and belief God will deliver us. Our relationships with Him will grow during those times of trials as a result. These circumstances may be debts left to pay from our lives of sin, or they may be new trials awaiting us in the future.

Just remember and believe that God will deliver you. You are the elect of God! Galatians 5:22–24 joins perfectly with Colossians 3:12 and further explains why God stresses to us, when in the early stages of our transformation, to rejoice and do good works (Ecclesiastes 3:12). God begins to cut away the roots that fed from the sinful world and replant roots that feed off His holy Word.

Increasing Love for Others

And may the Lord make you increase and abound in love to one another and to all, just as we do to you.—1 Thessalonians 3:12

The words in 1 Thessalonians 3:12 speak of abounding love toward one another. They speak of the Lord giving the increase for our love to abound toward all men. The relationship with our Lord Jesus Christ is the increase needed to make this possible. As we live our lives seeking Jesus's teachings and then putting them into action by our example, others will see the fruit and know to whom we belong. Jesus Christ set the example we all need to follow to receive the fruits of the Spirit and a love that grows toward all mankind—true love, not the love we have known while in bondage to the world and sin.

Love was always a selfish action to me before I knew Christ as my Lord and Savior. I judged love by what someone was willing to do for me, not by what I was willing to sacrifice for another. My love was lustful, prideful, controlling, and selfish. From my viewpoint today, my love at that time sounds a lot like fear and low self-esteem. Jesus Christ set the bar for love. Out of love, He took the cross for all of us, the most selfless act in the history of mankind. Christ sacrificed for all of us because of the ferocious love of the Father. Love was displayed upon the cross for all to see. Meekness, trust, humility, and plenty of long-suffering were the driving factors for Jesus Christ to follow the plan of love—the plan God had set forth for salvation of the world.

As we live a life founded on Jesus Christ, we will perform acts of love, selflessness, and kindness we never could have performed before. Our fruits also will be distributed to all those with whom we come into contact. Our examples of living a life based on the example of Christ will shine as a light for all to see. The fruits of the Spirit will illuminate our lights brighter over time. We can become loving—truly loving. We will not only learn to show love to those closest to us but in time, also to those we believed farthest away.

"By this all will know that you are My disciples, if you have love for one another" (John 13:35).

As a disciple of Christ and to truly transform our old persons of sin into new creations, we must be crucified along with Christ. We must die to our old lives and be reborn into our new lives. Death to the fear, guilt, pride, and selfishness we have known; life to mercy, kindness, humility, meekness, patience and, above all, love.

"I have been crucified with Christ; it is no longer I who live, but Christ lives in me; and the life which I now live in the flesh I live by faith in the Son of God, who loved me and gave Himself for me" (Galatians 2:20).

We are to seek to replicate the faith of our Lord as disciples of Christ. During our ongoing transformations, we continually will die to sin and further live in faith and Spirit. This is possible only through the love that has been shown us through Jesus Christ. By that love, we can lay down our lives as a sacrifice for others as well. Love, in God's terms, is impossible for us to comprehend. Thankfully, God's Word, from the very words of Jesus, gives us the outline needed to walk in love.

> As the Father loved Me, I also have loved you; abide in My love. If you keep My commandments, you will abide in My love, just as I have kept My Father's commandments and abide in His love. These things I have spoken to you, that My joy may remain in you, and that your joy may be full. This is My commandment, that you love one another as I have loved you. Greater love has no one than this, than to lay down one's life for his friends. You are My friends if you do whatever I command you. (John 15:9–14)

We see love repeated over and over again in John 15. Jesus tells us that the love He is seeking from us is our trust, faith, and obedience in Him. We can establish and build upon our love through the commandments He has commanded us. This will require our surrender to Him, our believing in Him, and our living for Him. Love, then, is being shown through laying down our lives and walking as instructed in newness of life, according to God's plans for us. We abide in the love of the Father and the Son and will be channels of that love to others. The love in which we partake will be increased through our personal lives and abound outward for all to see. As we begin to reflect God's heart with our own hearts, our love will drive us to intercede and help others, not just ourselves. Love will demand we make a difference in the lives of the afflicted and lost. Love will take us into volunteerism and circumstances of encouragement in which we once felt hopeless or perhaps not our concern. Love will keep us from hardening our hearts and minds. Love from God convicts our hearts and leads us away from sin. Make no mistake: love does not give us a free pass to live however we choose. Love brings us into living a joyous life as sons and daughters of the one true God as outlined by Him, not the world's shallow, false perversion on love.

"And above all things have fervent love for one another, for 'love will cover a multitude of sins'" (1 Peter 4:8).

This is the fight we are to take to the world. This is our weapon that we are given through Jesus Christ. Love is our power of Spirit to increase God's kingdom and see the sin of this world cleansed from the lives of its captives. Remember, we must love ourselves to ensure we do not again become one of those captives. How can we show love to others if we do not embrace God's love for us and love ourselves? Love casts out fears and doubts. Set aside your personal time of prayer and worship with the Lord and bask in that love. Continue to be reassured through God's Word confirming to you His love. Reflect God's love toward you and let the shadow of that love fall upon the hearts and lives of those around you.

Become Kind, Meek, and Merciful

How have you perceived meekness, humility, and long-suffering throughout your life?

_____
_____
_____
_____
_____
_____
_____
_____
_____
_____

Galatians 5:13–25 speaks directly to the fruits we will see come from the world and the fruits we will see come from the Spirit. Study these verses and define the worldly fruits and how we can separate our fruits from the world.

_____
_____
_____
_____
_____
_____
_____
_____
_____
_____

Increasing Love for Others

Explain the difference of love without Jesus Christ in your life and life as a follower of Jesus Christ.

Look at the following Scripture verses and relate their emphasis of love in your life.

Mark 12:28–31; John 14:21–24; 1 Corinthians 13; 1 John 4

_____

_____

_____

_____

_____

_____

_____

_____

_____

_____

_____

_____

Chapter 10

Living Your Life

Focus on God's Calling

> Now those who are such we command and exhort
> through our Lord Jesus Christ that they work in quietness
> and eat their own bread.—2 Thessalonians 3:12

Now we are entering an area of "Live" that will require deeper reflection and honesty, along with added prayer. The above verse from 2 Thessalonians 3:12 guides you to focus on your calling and direction from the Lord. Work in quietness and eat your own bread. What are we meant to see with this verse?

Before my new life in Christ, I had no knowledge of what this example of living meant. I focused on what my calling was in my mind. I also told everyone else what my calling was and what I felt their calling was. I was in everyone else's business and usually was consumed with plotting my victories and what others needed for their victories. There was no peace or direction for any involved. Let's look closer at the 3:11 verse that sets the tone for the message we are to see.

"For we hear that there are some who walk among you in a disorderly manner, not working at all, but are busybodies" (2 Thessalonians 3:11).

What a fitting verse to lead us into our 3:12 verse. The 3:11 verse perfectly explains who I once was and, if I let my selfish willpower lead me, who I become still today.

I was blind to the calling God had for me and not at all willing to eat the meal He had prepared. I lived in quest of controlling not only my life, but everyone else's live as well. I also was occupied for a big part of the day with outsmarting, out-calculating, and out-manipulating those by whom I felt threatened. I spent many a sleepless night with details from conversations, interactions, and appearances from others controlling my thoughts. I believed that if I could figure out the questions in my mind, as if some puzzle of wisdom that would place me in position of holding all the cards of knowledge, then all things could be made right. There was seldom a quiet moment in my mind. I was good at presenting the perception that I was calm, cool, and collected, but that was a lifelong rehearsal I acted out as a seasoned actor on the stage. My bread and plate set in front of me was by my own making, through endless expectations I created in my mind. I never felt satisfied after consuming what I had prepared for myself.

I focused on my perceptions, not on God's calling. Second Thessalonians 3:12 tells us to seek, be diligent, and be content of the calling and season in which God has placed us at the present time. God is our provider. God places the plate in front of us that He wishes us to eat at this time in our lives and at this stage of our transformations.

"I am the bread of life" (John 6:35).

Our bread is spiritual and rationed to us in measures of faith that coincide with our current calling and the season in which we are involved. Jesus must be our main focus and priority. We must consume His word and His truth and long for His grace and love before we will be able to perform any other calling or season in which we are placed.

Our first goal and love must be Jesus Christ. It must be personal with us before anything else.

Now, at times we may not be thrilled about the bread that is placed before us. Sometimes we need to go through some valleys in order to reach the mountain. The valleys can represent seasons in life when we do not see much spiritual growth. We may even question if our growth has ended or, worse yet, begun to regress. Do not be afraid. God has different lessons that we must learn, further removing the old to usher in the new. If we stand fast to our faith and live the life of a believer and a doer—a disciple—we will have plenty of times with the Lord on the mountaintops. In these times, the Father will provide a plentiful feast that will satisfy our souls. It is easy—and human nature—to return to mentalities that once were comfortable and part of who we believed ourselves to be. That is no longer us, my brothers and sisters in Christ. We are the called and chosen of God—saved and empowered to be finely refined treasures and warriors for the Lord. Our fruits of the Spirit will develop during these seasons. We must let them develop! How can we become trusting and peaceful if we are not willing to long-suffer for a time to attain what the Lord has in store for us? We confirm this through our faithfulness and by constantly seeking God in our everyday lives. We must have some sense of self-control and patience in order to be ushered into our next season. Let the working of our faith be steadfast and focus on what we are called to do at this present time. How can we receive the joy we hope for in the Lord if we are not willing to be obedient with the instructions and blessings we have at our current stage?

"His lord said to him, 'Well done, good and faithful servant; you were faithful over a few things, I will make you ruler over many things. Enter into the joy of your lord'" (Matthew 25:21).

"But seek first the kingdom of God and His righteousness, and all these things shall be added to you" (Matthew 6:33).

Be careful not to give in to the attacks of Satan. He will try to cloud your vision and once again return you to micromanaging your calling and everyone else's around you. As a result, you will spin your wheels and go backwards. You will accomplish nothing for God and usually will realize this fact after putting yourself through a sound humbling. We all have a different calling, as we have seen in 1 Kings 3:12. We need to be reassured God will lead us throughout the entire task at hand. Let our minds be at peace and perform the calling into which God has called us at the current time.

"Not that I speak in regard to need, for I have learned in whatever state I am, to be content" (Philippians 4:11).

Be content with God's plan, even when it does not match up with your time schedule or train of thought. Rejoice and do good for God. Be at peace and quietly accept what God provides. There will be plenty of times when our Father will give more than we can hold as well.

Lead as Christ Has Shown Us

> Let deacons be the husbands of one wife, ruling their children and their own houses well.—1 Timothy 3:12

Once we further accept living as Christ has shown, we can become resolved to fulfill the position in which He has placed us. First Timothy 3:12 speaks on deacons (elders, leaders of a local church body or congregation) and how they are to live. We may not be deacons of our churches at this point, but we are in various positions for God nonetheless. It makes no difference what those positions may be at this time; we are placed in them as representatives of disciples of Christ. We have scriptural guidance that leads us by God's Word in all these areas. For me, I hold the positions of: husband, father, son, employee, employer, leader of a ministry, member of a local church body, and member of the whole church body of Jesus Christ. God's Word gives one example after another for me to follow in order to fulfill my part in all these relationships and roles in which He has placed me. As a husband, I am told in Ephesians 5:23–33 to love my wife and sacrifice for her, just as Christ sacrificed Himself for His church. Ephesians 6 instructs me how to treat my children, parents, employer, and anyone who works for me. These are just a few examples of many throughout the Bible that guide us on our actions as followers of Christ. My point is that we all have responsibilities we are to fulfill, no matter our position in life.

As a father, a change took place in my home after I became a follower of Jesus Christ and recognized the changes that were required of me. I am the spiritual leader of my house. This is my God-given blessing, as well as my God-given responsibility.

"But as for me and my house, we will serve the Lord" (Joshua 24:15).

This is a wonderful verse from Joshua, but it is also a way of life to which we need to adhere, not just a quote or as mere words with no follow-up intentions. Dads, who do we have to blame when we hear our children use explicit sexual words among their friends or siblings? If we allow the viewing of television shows in our homes that promote this conduct, we can start by blaming ourselves. We can put parental controls on our televisions that make it impossible for anyone in our homes to watch the filth. We can communicate to our children that minds filled with all things ungodly will lead to ungodly things. If we make a decision to miss church so we can play in the baseball tournament every Sunday, how can we expect our families to prioritize church, now or any time in the future? If we spend all our time watching television and sports, how do we show our children to be involved with helping others? Below are a few examples of some of the excuses and pressures we will hear that attempt to sway us from the godly positions we hold.

* Would you deprive your children of that?
* All my friends' parents let them watch this show.
* I am too tired to go to church; I will watch it on TV and pray to God on my own.
* I deserve some "me time" on Sunday. I worked hard all week. It's my only day to relax.
* Everybody else is wearing this.

This is the mentality we are up against today. This was never God's mentality and still is not. Each one of us is faced with leading a life that sets an example for others. It is our choice to set the example God has already scripted for us or to go along with the way of the world and avoid any confrontations. Leading as Christ has shown us may very well place us in positions where the world wishes to disown us! We are called to do this nonetheless. We have been separated from the world, remember. We are the elect of God. The change we truly seek is not only for ourselves but for our families, coworkers, employers, schools, communities, and nation. Cycles must be broken if future generations are to avoid the same miserable outcome we faced before knowing Christ.

God is giving us new life. Along with a new life, new actions must follow. We will meet great resistance when we begin to live for God as He has instructed us to do. Be expecting it and stand firm. When children are involved, we need to explain why we are leading as we are. This gives us a wonderful opportunity to truly speak with them on our faith and salvation. We are not to become self-righteous judges with this phase of "Live." We can accomplish our Christ given roles with patience and love.

Over time, those around you will see your consistency and may even become curious about this new life you have chosen. You can lead with strength and still display love. You can respect God's Word and still remain respectful to those around you. Whatever position you are in, you can live a life based upon the convictions of your heart.

By this time in our transformation, our hearts will be convicted in pleasing and honoring God. Pray that God will give us the strength and encouragement needed to accomplish this new life. Pray that God will speak through us in the positions of life we hold. It all starts with each one of us. Do we wish to fall back into lives of compromise and negligence to our Creator and His plans for us? If we do, we fail God in this new life of salvation and glimpse of grace He has offered. We cannot pick and choose which Scriptures we like and which Scriptures to pass on because of how the world will respond. We not only fail our God, but we also fail all those around us.

Husbands, do you want to fail your wives and become casualties in the long death of marriage to which this world has become numb? Dads, do you want to fail your children and set the example for your children to one day repeat of a father consumed with the world? Employees, do you want to work honestly and respectfully for the blessings and jobs God provides through your employers or slip into another case of entitlement, mediocrity, and constant strife toward your careers? We need to lead by the example of Jesus Christ. We are given new lives, new hope, and the same responsibilities we always had but to which we just never responded.

This phase will require further trust and communication through prayer with God. This area of change in life will not be easy. God promises us He will guide us by the Holy Spirit and supply our every need. God also promises us that the world will attack us and persecute us. The world may even hate us for our faith and beliefs. In the next chapter, we will dive into this subject much deeper and prepare ourselves for the trials that lie ahead.

Focus on God's Calling

What do you believe your current calling is from the Lord? Where do you feel your focus should be at this current time and season?

_____

_____

_____

_____

_____

_____

_____

_____

_____

_____

_____

_____

_____

Look at the following verses and relate how they speak to you with regard to focusing on your own personal calling: Matthew 7:3–5; Revelation 2:1–5.

_____

_____

_____

_____

_____

_____

_____

_____

_____

_____

_____

Read John 6:48–58 and describe where we receive our true Bread of Life.

_____

_____

_____

_____

_____

_____

_____

_____

_____

_____

_____

_____

Lead as Christ Has Shown Us

List the current positions you hold and how you can fulfill these as a disciple of Jesus Christ.

_____

_____

_____

_____

_____

_____

_____

_____

_____

_____

_____

_____

Look at the following Scripture readings and describe what they say as leading, according to God's Word: Deuteronomy 6:4–9; Ephesians 5; Ephesians 6:1–9.

_____

_____

_____

_____

_____

_____

_____

_____

_____

_____

_____

_____

Chapter 11

Persecutions and Trials

Yes, and all who desire to live godly in Christ Jesus
will suffer persecution.—2 Timothy 3:12

When we not only hear the Word of God but also live the words of God, our new lives in Christ will be very rewarding for the mind, body, and soul. We will grow stronger in faith and further in Christ each day we focus upon God's calling for us. We will truly be an example of the elect of God. God's Holy Spirit will separate us from the rest of the world and how we live life.

Second Timothy 3:12 tells us if we live our lives as Jesus Christ taught us, we will suffer persecution. These persecutions will come in many different forms and from various places. Some persecutions will come from where we least expect them and from whom we least expect. Others will try to discourage, downplay, and disregard our faith in Christ. We will be under attack on a constant basis when we become a voice for Christ. Jesus speaks to His apostles and those around Him and tells them:

"And you will be hated by all for My name's sake. But he who endures to the end will be saved" (Matthew 10:22).

Today, the world where we live often hates us for Jesus's sake. I spoke in earlier chapters on how Satan pretty well has the world in chaos and complete blindness to God's will for the inhabitants of earth. The gospel of John, chapter 1, speaks on this issue. Jesus Christ is the light. John 1:5, 10 explains the darkness not comprehending the light and the world not knowing Him. The world was full of sin, death, and darkness before Jesus Christ took the form of man and became the sacrifice for man to receive that light in his heart. Without Jesus Christ, we cannot come to the light and salvation of God. Our souls before knowing Jesus Christ as our Lord and Savior are in darkness—darkness inhabited with sin, captivity, remorse, lies, deceit, and fear. Once we receive Jesus into our hearts and begin a new life in Him, the light begins to chase away the dark. Those remaining around us who have not received the light of Christ will not comprehend our transformation. Regrettably, most of this world does not comprehend that light.

Second Timothy 3:12 tells us that as a receiver of that beautiful light of Christ, be prepared for the persecutions of this world. Jesus tells us in Matthew, chapter 5, that we are blessed and should rejoice when the world persecutes us for His sake. Let's be honest; it is hard to be joyful when we are being persecuted. Why would Jesus tell us such a thing? Surely God knows that it goes against all human nature to be positive and happy when under attack or when we feel like outsiders looking in. Jesus tells us this for the spiritual nature, not the human nature. When we are criticized for our Christian life, then we obviously are giving the example of a Christian life that others clearly see. Others, who live for the world and the treasures thereof, will feel threatened or superior to a Christian life. People can be very defensive toward what they do not understand. I will again use myself as an example.

I am not at all proud of this example, but I feel I must be honest so others can one day be honest as well. And although I am not proud of this, I am forgiven. Before giving my life to Jesus Christ, I was a huge critic of anyone who had taken that step. I really viewed giving one's life to Jesus Christ as an excuse for a person to give up in life and cease dealing with reality. I believed people had become so unwilling to fight for their own beliefs that they took the easy way out. I viewed these people as being guilty of horrible things, people who they realized their only hope to ever be forgiven was to start proclaiming Jesus. I viewed these people as weak and often pathetic.

As I said, I am not at all proud of this view I lived under before knowing Christ. I will tell you, however, as I am writing this, I cannot help but laugh at myself and be amazed by how God used His wisdom to deal with me. My views were exactly right in most cases but completely misunderstood in my heart. I was right—most people had no way out and finally gave up and gave their lives to Jesus. I had no way out of the misery and anxiety I was experiencing in the days leading up to my surrendering to Christ. I had no fight left in me whatsoever. I had done horrible things and was guilty of inflicting great pain on others. I had become one of those weak and pathetic souls I used to persecute. Thank God I was one of those people!

The perceptions in my mind and the lies of Satan to which he has the world in bondage fight against us, right up to the very moment of surrender to Christ. Once we have surrendered, the perceptions in our minds begin changing, but the perceptions of those who do not know Christ remain the same. This transformation God performs through us should become a major contrast to the world of which Satan is in command. As this contrast becomes more apparent, expect the persecutions to increase. Friends who could always rely upon you to help out with an inappropriate good time will see you no longer partake in things you once did. This will leave them confused and angry. They will believe you are turning your back on them or think you are too good for them, now that you're such a holy-roller.

Coworkers who were accustomed to hearing our filthy mouths will be baffled by the fact we do not talk that way as much—and hopefully one day, not at all. There will be extreme opposition by the groups of people with the "anything goes" attitude, which so much of this world shares. We will be seen as insensitive, unapproachable, and uncivilized. God gives us very clear dos and don'ts in the Bible. We will live this life for others to see, and those who do not wish to follow the dos and don'ts will not like the fact that we are following. Then, there will be persecutions from the areas we don't expect. Family members who are not saved will be unable to grasp this newfound hope we have. They may accuse us of being false or putting on an act out of desperation. I can assure the husbands who read this book that a wife who has seen year after year of a selfish husband probably won't sing for joy the moment he tells her of his salvation. Our nearest loved ones may even unknowingly be one of our main areas of persecution in the beginning. Be patient; it will pass with time. Simply stay surrendered and see the final outcome through faith, not through today's catastrophe.

We must not underestimate that Satan will persecute us as well. Satan will come after us with all he has. We may suffer the loss of jobs, finances, and possessions. We may be placed in positions with non-Christians who might attack us on a daily basis. Satan will work endlessly to penetrate our minds with doubts and regrets. Satan has alcohol, drugs, sex, greed, pride, and vanity to lure people into performing his work. Satan believes if the cost is too high for us to remain faithful, we will cash it all in and return to his forces, along with the world we once knew. *Satan is a liar!* He does not wish to give us eternal life in paradise. In order to see the eternity of being in the presence of God, we must identify that the persecutions of this short life will pass. At one time in my life, I could only see a few years down the road. I prioritized only those that would bring me gain in this world. Surrendering my life to Jesus Christ has made me a visionary. I now see the future eternity God has promised me. This life will pass, and all we know of this world will perish. Jesus Christ is preparing a mansion for us in the kingdom of heaven—that mansion will remain forever.

I will not tell you that I am overcome with joy during persecutions and trials. Oftentimes through my own pain and stubbornness, God reveals yet another lesson for me to learn that brings me closer to Jesus, my Savior. I merely will tell you to look upon the example Jesus Christ gave us. Jesus underwent more persecution than any of us will ever imagine. Jesus was arrested, beaten, scourged, and crucified. We do not understand persecution such as what our Lord went through. Through it all, He remained surrendered and obedient to God. In some parts of this world, being a Christian can bring persecution that will cost the believer his or her life. This loss of life is tragic and wrong, but look at the example these saints are leaving for us. I can hear their spirits talking to us. I will stand for my belief in Jesus Christ, my Lord. He stood for me!

"I will not leave you orphans; I will come to you" (John 14:18).

"These things I have spoken to you, that in Me you may have peace. In the world you will have tribulation; but be of good cheer, I have overcome the world" (John 16:33).

"Because you have kept My command to persevere, I also will keep you from the hour of trial that shall come upon the whole world, to test those who dwell on the earth" (Revelation 3:10).

Once surrendered, believed, and living, we become a soldier for Jesus Christ. Persecutions will come from many diverse places, along with those who dwell in darkness and from Satan as well. If there is any reason to feel blessed and rejoice, I believe it is the following: living for Jesus Christ and His teachings has placed us in a position to suffer as our Lord had to suffer. How better to know we are on the path of righteousness than to suffer for a time for the One who suffered for all. Jesus tells us to rejoice in the Spirit. We are on the right path to spend eternity with Him!

Persecutions and Trials

How do you plan to defend yourself from persecutions and trials? Study the following verses and use them to help prepare your heart and mind.

Ephesians 6:12–20; James 1

_____

_____

_____

_____

_____

_____

_____

_____

_____

_____

_____

_____

_____

Chapter 12

No Turning Back

Warning for Unbelief

> Beware, brethren, lest there be in any of you an evil heart of unbelief in departing from the living God.—Hebrews 3:12

As we approach the end phase of "Live" in *3:12 Transformation,* God reminds us to remain faithful, believe in our hearts, and be completely on fire for Christ. Hebrews 3:12 is a warning to us that we could return to our past bondage if our hearts do not remain believing.

Hebrews speaks how God worked through Moses to lead His people out of Egypt and how the people, once again, hardened their hearts. They failed to see and believe all God had done for them. As a result of their disbelieving hearts, Israel spent forty years wandering in the desert.

"So I swore in My wrath they shall not enter My rest" (Hebrews 3:11).

How could the people of Israel turn away from God? God freed them from bondage, parted the Red Sea for their escape, and closed it again for the destruction of their enemy. He provided food and water for them and guided their path with His presence. How could people's hearts be hardened after such salvation by God Himself? The answer is their unbelief.

As earlier stated in this book, I hold fast to belief being our biggest success or failure along the way of our transformations. How does belief affect the way we live? We will live the way we believe. If we feel in our hearts that an action would be wrong in the sight of God, and we choose not to act upon it as a result, we are living by God's presence in faith. If we choose to do things that go against God, but we do not believe any consequences will come—or we just don't care—we have hardened our hearts to the Lord. I was forgiven for all my sins and led from the bondage of sin and addictions. I have never gone without food, clothing, and shelter. God has given me a vision and a work to perform for His kingdom to be spread and His Son to be glorified. In my testimony and before my very eyes, God reunited my family and marriage and placed peace and joy in my heart that I'd never imagined. God has been so gracious and merciful. Could I ever become hardened and unbelieving? Could you? The answer for both of us is yes.

All we do needs to be done with gratefulness and remembrance of what God has done for us. God needs to be our first love. As soon as priorities change in our lives, our relationship with God will change as well. God has to be the number one priority—number one, before wives, husbands, work, children, money, sports, etc. If we call upon God only when we need Him, I believe God will feel like He is no longer our priority and first love. If we thank God for the miracle but then go about living life selfishly and however we choose, we will hear these words from Jesus one day:

"I never knew you" (Matthew 7:23).

This departing from God sounds like it would be a huge decision. We would have to be consciously involved in such a decision that affected our lives, right? Not at all! This departing from our Lord is usually subtle and in the form of baby steps. We slowly begin consulting less with God in prayer and worship. We give too much time to our thoughts and plans, rather than seeking God's plan for us. We become more believing in our own abilities and resources and less seeking of God's. These signs, in early stages, do not set off an alarm that notifies fellow Christians—alarms with screaming high tones alerting the need of spiritual counsel and accountability. These are signs that our minds need to see early. If we fail to see the signs or choose to ignore them, our hearts partake in turning away from God as well. Then we will reach a stage where our fellow brothers and sisters also clearly see our signs of disbelief. Our actions will reflect what our hearts and minds are being consumed with. We will depart from the living God through disbelief once again.

It must have been heartbreaking, mixed with furious anger, for God to see His children, whom He had led out of slavery from Egypt, seeking to return again to Egypt. They were not willing to wait, trust, and believe upon the Lord for their every provision and protection. Fear overpowered their faith, and therefore they wished to journey back to Egypt. Sure, they were going to assume the role of oppressed slaves again, but this was a role with which they were familiar; one where they knew their purpose and had an existence. Israel forgot the power God had showed them and the provision He had supplied. Israel was willing to compromise their true identity as God's chosen people. They were unbelieving that God would continue to be with them and fight their battles for them. Moses, Caleb, and Joshua all tried to convince the people to trust in God, that He would provide their every need and give them the

Promised Land of which He had spoken. But unfortunately, they did not surrender, believe, or live as God instructed. Their season in the desert was prolonged through their hardened hearts of disbelief. Many—all but two—never entered into the Promised Land. Only Caleb and Joshua, through their belief, entered.

God's heart mourns no less today for His children, who begin walking and following His Son only to stray away from His guidance through disbelief; who begin to feel and experience God's love and presence but refuse to latch on to that promise of love for evermore. His beloved children will not listen to the current Moseses, Calebs, or Joshuas the Lord has provided to guide and encourage them. They break away from the safety of fellowshipping and prayer and return to isolation, where they feel lost and abandoned again. In time, the bondage from which they have been freed (their modern-day Egypt) begins looking fairly safe again. At least they know what to expect, and they again have an identity—a false identity the Enemy gave them but an identity nonetheless. They will wander again throughout their desert and more than likely never enter their Promised Land.

Our intimate relationship with God is on the line if we do not strangle any oxygen from the neck of disbelief as soon as it gasps for air. Seek guidance from God daily. Today, if you hear His voice, harden not your hearts.

"For we have become partakers of Christ if we hold the beginning of our confidence steadfast to the end" (Hebrews 3:14).

All In for Jesus

Can a fig tree, my brethren, bear olives, or a grapevine bear figs? Thus no spring yields both salt water and fresh.—James 3:12

Our confidence began when we accepted Jesus Christ into our hearts. We asked Him into our hearts with brokenness, humility, hope, faith, and longing for His presence to guide us. If we stand fast with that desire in our lives every day and live that example, we will not harden our hearts. James 3:12 further reinforces the all in for Jesus Christ lifestyle we need to live. Can a spring yield both freshwater and saltwater? Our souls are a spring for God. These springs should flow with freshwater that will sustain us and give refreshment to others for the Lord. Our spring also can bring forth saltwater if we choose to live a life of sin. Saltwater will overtake any freshwater in our streams and try to contaminate the water of others as well.

"He who believes in Me, as the Scripture has said, out of his heart will flow rivers of living water" (John 7:38).

When we seek the Lord's guidance, our spring flows with the direction of the Holy Spirit. Living waters come from Jesus Christ. Our waters from Christ will refresh us when we're thirsty and quench us when we're dry. If our springs are of salt and sin, we cannot maintain life in Christ. Our waters not only will lead to our deaths, but they also will give no refreshment to those around us. Chapter 3 of James also speaks of our tongues, which we can use to proclaim our Lord or profane our Lord. We can bless our fellow brothers and sisters with our words or murder them with our words. Our tongue is so small, yet we use it as if it is larger than God. Cease attacking one another! Hateful and cruel words are launched in attacks to destroy each other's joy, cause fear, promote anger, and cause dissension. These are shameful words of death used to further kill the hopes, dreams, and beliefs of others. Our belittling of others may cause laughter among our peers. Our filthy words that focus on vulgarity and profanity are confession of our giving in to lust and wicked thoughts. Jesus tells us to give praise and thanks to our Father. Witness to others what God has done with encouragement and love. Bless others with prayers to God. Let God's Word flow from your tongue. Use your God-given gift of speech to give God's good news to others! We must be all in! There is no middle ground, my brothers and sisters. We cannot go forward in Christ with the weights and cares of this world holding us back. The 3:12 Transformation constantly prepares us with the verse the Lord reveals to move forward in faith and confidence into the next verse and phase He has ready.

Hebrews 11:13–16 talks about strangers and pilgrims. These verses speak of confession, witness, and testimony of the faithful elect of God, who seek a country built through foundational truths and heavenly principles. This is unattainable with true friendship with the world, longing for acceptance of the world, and fear of being left out of what the world offers us. This country is not existent in the present world of which we are a part. The lie to which we all too often fell victim was that we could possibly attain our heart's desires and peace through anything the world offers. Our time upon the earth is short, but our selfish demands and fears of our flesh are great. Our heavenly Father knew we would struggle with this. His hopes for our victory are why He sacrificed His Son in order to ensure our inheritance with Him in the country we truly seek. But first we must identify that our longing for peace and security cannot be sufficed by this world. Second, our only possible way to overcome the flesh is through the Spirit of Christ. Third, through growing faith, we must further crucify our flesh, which continually struggles to return us to the country we have left behind.

I love the phrase "burn the ships" more and more. I am learning with each day that the ship that brought us to where God has called and chosen us could return us to the country we knew before knowing

Jesus Christ. The ship truly is constructed out of physical and spiritual materials that can quietly sneak back up and reconstruct a vessel, prepared to launch across the ocean of salvation with the destination of worldly treasures on the horizon. We are the builders of the ship. Any remaining parts that remain washed up on the beach of faith we have encountered will continue to move in and out with the tides of trials and unexpected persecutions of this world and life. They will bang against our shores with the haunting memory of the wreck, which led us to our first arrival. Only faith of the inheritance, which lies ahead when we spiritually view the terrain, can keep us from humanely looking back across the ocean where we may have once seemed assured and grounded in our worldly inhabitants. If we stare too long across the ocean, we may gather some of the rubble together once again and build our ships with the unknowing preparation of setting across the ocean to a more comfortable, accepted, and successful fellowship with the world. We begin by building a hull from any leftover pieces of selfishness lying on the beach. Then some nice thick sections of fear make a great stem for cutting through any difficult moral issues that could arise in the form of waves to stop our ship from sailing. Pride and foolishness are a wonderful combination for a solid stern and a fitting last image for those remaining on the beach as we sail into the abyss. And of course, let's not forget our sails and mast that are driven by disbelief, lack of patience, and immediate need for personal gratification.

When our vessel of destruction first hits the beach of salvation, we need to get out and set fire to the ship immediately! Sometimes we get worried about the rough terrain the spiritual world holds in store, and we run to extinguish the flames coming from our ships, hoping to leave an escape route, if needed. Then again, even when the main body of the ship has been burned, some smaller pieces may have been washed to shore and buried under the sand at first.

These are not noticed at the start but eventually will surface and then show life in the country we have left and a willingness to be reconstructed if the owner will submit to working with these pieces. We need to understand a small fire is necessary at this time. Perhaps the big fire took care of the main vessel, but little fires cannot be overlooked when needed. If we don't burn the ship and all remaining remnants when they surface, how can we ever truly eliminate our return to the world and confess our relentless pursuit of our Lord? Only then can we each say, "I am a stranger and pilgrim to this earth." My country is yet to come, but some remnants that cannot be burned remain within me in the form of the true living God. That is the vessel to which I will dedicate my spiritual life reconstruction. And I will pray the Father will, at all times, be my master builder.

Our lives need to be lived by this example. We are believers in Jesus Christ and consistently will follow His teachings in life. We no longer are in the utterly broken stage as when we first accepted Jesus into our hearts. If in the first transformational stages, we can expect some salt to mix into the freshwater at times. But once surrendered and believing and living a life for Christ, there has to be zealousness in our hearts for Jesus. Hold yourself to a higher standard in Jesus. Expect to be that spring that can give another soul the thirst-quenching witnessing needed at the time. Live for Jesus, by Jesus, and according to Jesus. Give all you have for God each day! Do not compromise that which God has spoken to you! Surrender, believe, and live what Jesus Christ has done and the life He sets for you to live. Then, you will be ready to take the next phase of 3:12 Transformation—the area of your life for which Jesus Christ gave His life so all could hear the good news!

Warning for Unbelief

What could be possible warning signs that you are departing from God's presence in your life?

_____

_____

_____

_____

_____

_____

_____

_____

_____

_____

Look at the following Scripture verses. Speak on the people's disbelief and hardening of their hearts: Exodus 14:11; Numbers 14:1–4; Numbers 21:5; Hebrews 3:7–19.

_____

_____

_____

_____

_____

_____

_____

_____

_____

_____

All In for Jesus

What is your willingness to be all in for Jesus Christ in your life? What do you think this requires?

_____

_____

_____

_____

_____

_____

_____

_____

_____

_____

_____

_____

Proclaim

Chapter 13

Proclaim Your Faith and Hope

Proclaim God's Faithfulness

> So He said, "I will certainly be with you. And this
> shall be a sign to you that I have sent you: When
> you have brought the people out of Egypt, you shall
> serve God on this mountain." —Exodus 3:12

Now we are entering into service for the Lord. Proclaim the good news of salvation! Jesus Christ died, was buried, and rose again. After Christ's resurrection, He ascended to the Father. We who believe become the example of Christ on earth after that point. Those who have been given mercy will give mercy. Those who have been set free will freely give to others. Those who know Christ will introduce Him to those who do not.

The first verse of this phase, "Proclaim," is Exodus 3:12. This particular verse ties the entire 3:12 Transformation message into perfect oneness. In Exodus 3, God speaks to Moses through a burning bush. God tells Moses how He has seen the oppression of His people in Egypt and plans to deliver them out of captivity. God informs Moses that he will go to Egypt and be the one God has chosen to lead the Israelites out of captivity. In Exodus 3:12,

Moses is reassured that God will be present with him. God gives Moses a sign for the future that will manifest itself once Moses has followed God's word. God sends Moses into Egypt to proclaim the freedom and liberty of God's people. Moses is to proclaim this to the Israelites, all the people of Egypt, and Pharaoh, the king. In Exodus 4, Moses doubts, questions, and asks God to choose someone else. Moses had to surrender to God's will, believe God would be with him, and live as God instructed him; then he was able to proclaim to God's people and all of Egypt that the new season of freedom from oppression was at hand.

We all have similar stages to go through, as Moses did. All our efforts and learning to walk as Christ has shown us leads to this point of our transformations.

"For you were bought at a price; therefore glorify God in your body and in your spirit, which are God's" (1 Corinthians 6:20).

The purchase price for our sins and lives of bondage was the blood of Jesus Christ. The purchase that we all receive through faith is salvation in Christ. The price for us is to proclaim that purchase to others for the glory of God. In Exodus 3:12, what God is telling us, in my words, is as follows: "Go forth and spread the message of salvation. I will be with you. You will lead others to freedom, and they shall worship My name. I will show you My faithfulness."

When God first gave me the vision of 3:12 Transformation through my dream, I was excited and hopeful. Within a few days, I shared the dream with my pastor, Jeff Rasanen. Some time was spent praying for God's guidance, researching the verses, and weighing the options for this message to become a recovery group at our church. After three to four months, Pastor Jeff and I met again. I had developed some paperwork and a rough outline for the program.

Pastor Jeff asked me again to pray on the matter and also gave me other information pertaining to other options for existing recovery groups. Our church had been seeking a recovery program for some time but was waiting for the right one and a willing volunteer to commit to it. Pastor Jeff asked me to look over the other programs, look over 3:12 Transformation, and decide which program to start at our church. He also gave me complete support and said he would trust my decision.

I had received the vision months earlier and was confident while preparing that with which God had led me. All of a sudden, when faced with the decision of 3:12 Transformation or another existing group, I seemed to doubt for a short time. I felt a sense of fear that no one would listen to me. I realized beginning a new recovery program, whether based solely on Jesus Christ or not, was near impossible with all the existing programs that already had a following and an established name. I worried my church, Pastor Jeff, and I would be made to look like fools when the program crashed and burned. With a broken heart, I talked myself into not risking it and going with an existing spiritually based recovery program. After all, I wanted to help others find hope. It didn't matter whether or not it was my program; it only had to be God's program. I decided to look at the chapter 3s and verse 12s once again. I was trying to find peace on the issue. I prayed to God and asked for His guidance and my acceptance, no matter what His will was.

Originally, 3:12 Transformation had fifteen verses. There were certain verses I did not recognize at first or did not feel they related to recovery. After the prayer to God for direction and guidance, I sat down once again and opened the Bible. I would go through all sixty-six books of the Bible again and was determined to make my decision. God gave me the answer, confirmation, and calling my spirit was longing to hear! In the second book of the Bible, Exodus

3:12 came to life to me. This was one of the verses I didn't see originally as pertaining to recovery. God used this verse to be my burning bush. It was time to truly see God's calling in my life. The calling was to proclaim God's message to others. Fear of failure vanished. Questioning how I'd be received by others was no longer a thought. The promise God gave was that people in bondage would be freed, and they would come to worship Him. I faithfully believed that promise with all my heart. God launched me into proclamation at this point. There was no turning back after that day. I went to Pastor Jeff with boldness and confidence that 3:12 Transformation was the program for our church. I became willing to lead others and put my reputation and story out in the public for the world to see, regardless of the outcome.

How do I explain my time of doubt? I have come to believe that period was needed in my journey with the Lord. I believe God wanted to see my desire to serve Him exclusively and the importance this placed upon my soul. God wanted to see me exhaust my human thought process so He could show me His message. It was a faith builder and promise God wanted me to see at that very time in my life. God wants us to proclaim of what we have been recipients. God will show each and every one of us our calling and the perfect time to proclaim that calling. Once we receive that confirmation from the Lord, we will proclaim with boldness and confidence our hopes, turned into faith and true belief!

Let's look at God's messenger Moses closer. Through God's presence and power, Moses brought forth ten plagues on the people of Egypt, which showed God's presence with Israel. Moses separated the Red Sea, which gave safe passage to Israel and then destroyed the Egyptians. Through God's provision, Moses was the intercessor for Israel in the wilderness for forty years; interceding for the people's sin, requests for food and water, guidance and leadership from the Lord, and protection and victory through wars. Moses was the recipient of God's Ten Commandments, which established the law and outline for Israel to live. What a great man of faith! He was chosen and empowered by God to lead His people out of bondage and into their Promised Land. Wouldn't you love to have faith like Moses had? But let's look closer at Moses's beginnings. Moses was spared from the Egyptians as an infant. The pharaoh of Egypt was fearful that the Israelite people were growing too strong and large. Pharaoh felt that Israel could overpower Egypt and depart to another nation and war against them. Pharaoh gave the order to kill all the newborn sons of Israel in an attempt to control their numbers and break their spirits. He had them thrown into the Nile River to die.

Moses was born during this time. His mother and father were not willing to let their son be killed; they believed God had a plan and purpose for their son. His parents fashioned a basket, laid Moses in it, and placed the basket floating in the Nile. As God would have it, Moses was indeed spared. Pharaoh's daughter found the young infant in the basket and claimed him as her own son. Moses was raised in Egypt and in the very house of Pharaoh, the man who declared death to all the other infants such as Moses. God's relationship and protection of His son Moses was established from the beginning.

Then, when Moses was grown, he saw an Egyptian wrongfully beating a Hebrew. Now, according to Hollywood, Moses rushed in to stop the wrongful persecution and, in the heat of the moment, accidentally killed the Egyptian. Fearing for his life, he fled from Egypt, or (depending upon which movie you're watching) he was banished from the land of Egypt as a traitor. This depiction is not exactly the way the Word of God depicts the historic events.

> Now it came to pass in those days, when Moses was grown, that he went out to his brethren and looked at their burdens. And he saw an Egyptian beating a Hebrew, one of his brethren. *So he looked this way and that way, and when he saw no one, he killed the Egyptian and hid him in the sand.* And when he went out the second day, behold, two Hebrew men were fighting, and he said to the one who did the wrong, "Why are you striking your companion?" Then he said, "Who made you a prince and a judge over us? Do you intend to kill me as you killed the Egyptian?" So *Moses feared and said, "Surely this thing is known!"* When Pharaoh heard of this matter, he sought to kill Moses. *But Moses fled* from the face of Pharaoh and dwelt in the land of Midian; and he sat down by a well. (Exodus 2:11–15, italics added)

As we see from God's Word, Moses not only contemplated the murder but made sure no one would see his actions. He also took efforts to hide what he had done from everyone around him. Then, when he realized his actions were known, he feared for his life and fled the situation. Unfortunately, I can very much relate to Moses. Many times I acted exactly the same way in my life of sin and selfishness. I could not let anyone see the actions I was about to take. I tried with all my manipulative, deceitful efforts to keep my actions from being known by those around me. Once busted, my fear of what penalties lay ahead often caused me to flee from the situation and not deal with it. Or I would once again make promises that I would eventually break. Oh yes, I can definitely relate to this early Moses. But then, God did something amazing in Moses's life. He led him into a new land. Moses took a wife and became a shepherd. One day, while tending his flock, he saw an amazing sight—a bush that was burning, but the bush was not consumed by the fire. Moses decided to look closer at this amazing sight to try to comprehend what was happening.

> And the Angel of the LORD appeared to him in a flame of
> fire from the midst of a bush. So he looked, and behold,
> the bush was burning with fire, but the bush was not
> consumed. Then Moses said, "I will now turn aside and
> see this great sight, why the bush does not burn." So when
> the LORD saw that he turned aside to look, God called to
> him from the midst of the bush and said, "Moses, Moses!"
> And he said, "Here I am." Then He said, "Do not draw
> near this place. Take your sandals off your feet, for the
> place where you stand is holy ground." (Exodus 3:2–5)

What took place in Moses's life at this time? He acknowledged the
Lord and His calling upon his life. When God saw that He had
Moses's attention, the Lord then could clearly speak to him in an
intimate relationship—the relationship God had in store for Moses
all along. God then told Moses to remove the sandals from his feet,
for the ground he was now upon was holy ground.

In no way do I wish to make Moses appear as anything other than a
great man of faith. I truly wish to have faith like Moses's. However,
I am using his life for all of us to be encouraged—his life before
the burning bush. I can sense the desperation, anger, and fear in
Moses as I read Exodus 2. Undoubtedly, he must have felt like life
was pretty much over. What good could possibly come from his
time in Egypt? He must have undergone loneliness and isolation
while fleeing for his life. But none of this disqualified Moses from
fulfilling—or should I say, proclaiming—the purpose for which God
created him. God knew of Moses's past. He also knew all of Moses's
future. For Moses to believe his future was no longer based upon
his past, God instructed him to remove his sandals, for the ground
he would walk upon was holy ground. We, as Moses, have been
ushered into this holy ground as well. Our past has not and will not
disqualify us from the love and purpose of our heavenly Father—our

God! The same God who called Moses from the burning bush, now the God of heaven and earth, has called us!

However ugly our lives or however broken the trail that is left from our past, we now have a new future and destiny through Jesus Christ. Through surrender, believing, living, and proclaiming our newfound life and hope in Jesus, we will proclaim to the world the freedom of God's people. Don't be surprised if you see waters divided, mountains moved, or the dead come to life. You are on God's holy ground and journey now—the journey of proclaiming freedom and liberty to all who will acknowledge their burning bush when God calls!

Boldly Proclaim New Hope to Others

> Therefore, since we have such hope, we use great
> boldness of speech.—2 Corinthians 3:12

Second Corinthians 3:12 tells us to boldly proclaim new hope to others. That is exactly what we are to do—spread hope and good news. Proclaim to others how they can receive the same peace, joy, and salvation we have come to know by knowing Jesus Christ.

"The Spirit of the Lord God is upon Me, because the Lord has anointed Me to preach good tidings to the poor; He has sent Me to heal the brokenhearted, to proclaim liberty to the captives, and the opening of the prison to those who are bound" (Isaiah 61:1).

The above verse in Isaiah is a prophecy of the words that would be spoken by Christ the Messiah. Jesus Christ fulfills this prophecy in Luke 4:17–21. We are the ones to carry this message and continue representing Christ in this day and age. Through our testimony, we are given power through the Holy Spirit to relay this message. We are commissioned by God to preach the gospel, heal the brokenhearted, proclaim liberty to the captives, and free those oppressed. Jesus Christ is alive—Jesus was, is, and always will be. We have become the disciples of Christ and are now responsible for proclaiming salvation to the broken and lost.

When you go out and witness to others, do it with conviction and belief of what you have experienced. Put passion and love in your heart when proclaiming Jesus. We have been freed and given God's anointing to carry on the work of Christ. To how many brothers and sisters will we give hope if we sound unsure and complacent? Now, I realize this will be a process. Actively pray to God and the Holy Spirit to increase your proclaiming and boldness in Christ. Trust what God has shown you thus far. Your proclaiming is God's glorification. God will guide you.

The apostles of Jesus Christ give us a true example of transformation and boldness in which we all can take comfort. On the night Jesus was betrayed, all the apostles abandoned Him. They ran away into hiding to protect themselves. Peter denied Jesus three times on the night He was arrested and taken into custody. I can only imagine the utter fear and anxiety the apostles must have undergone. The shame and guilt of their betrayal of Christ, to which they must have been subject, could have been nothing less than overbearing upon their spirits. The man they knew to be the Son of God, to whom all their hopes and beliefs were given, was taken from them and condemned in a single night. The next day, they would have heard all the reports of how their Master had been beaten, scourged, ridiculed, and mocked. Then they would be told that Jesus had been crucified, and He died upon the cross. He was taken down and laid in a tomb, and a stone was rolled in front of it. It would have been hard not to give up at this time in their lives—ashamed, guilt-ridden, broken, and scared. Life would have seemed useless to continue for the apostles. What good could possibly come of such tragic events?

Jesus rose from the grave three days later! In God's wonderful, mysterious way, the first recorded transformations of broken people had begun. The apostles were forgiven. They saw, firsthand, God's gift of grace through Jesus Christ. The chains of bondage that held the apostles from going forward boldly had been shattered. Their darkness was turned into light. Salvation had come to the followers of Christ! The world attempted to kill Jesus Christ and place Him in the grave for eternity. But Jesus Christ conquered the grave for all His followers to spend eternity with Him. Forty days later, Jesus Christ ascended into heaven with the Father. He instructed His apostles to remain in Jerusalem and wait for His promise. He promised to send His Holy Spirit to them.

"But you shall receive power when the Holy Spirit has come upon you: and you shall be witnesses to Me in Jerusalem, and in all Judea and Samaria, and to the end of the earth" (Acts 1:8).

When the apostles received the Holy Spirit, as promised, there was a dramatic transformation in their lives. These once-broken men who ran away from the Lord were now given power and boldness. They were given wisdom and faith. They were given the words to proclaim and testify of Jesus Christ and witness what had taken place in their lives. Peter, who had denied Christ three times, stood up on the day of Pentecost and boldly proclaimed Jesus Christ. As a result of Peter's transformation and power through the Holy Spirit, his proclaiming Jesus Christ led three thousand souls to repentance and belief in Jesus on that same day. Other apostles went on to write Gospels contained in the Bible (John, Matthew). The apostles proclaimed the good news of Jesus Christ throughout the region. By their testimonies, others carried the message of Christ and salvation also. Then others became partakers in the proclaiming. As a result, the apostles of Jesus, once seemingly lost and without guidance, turned the world upside down through the Holy Spirit of God—the Holy Spirit that revealed to them how to proclaim boldly the new hope and life they had been given.

"But the anointing which you have received from Him abides in you, and you do not need that anyone teach you; but as the same anointing teaches you concerning all things, and is true, and is not a lie, and just as it has taught you, you will abide in Him" (1 John 2:27).

God's Holy Spirit will be your teacher. You may be led to others for God's Word and guidance as well. Just believe that God will give you the boldness, confidence, and words to proclaim and magnify His holy name.

Proclaim God's Faithfulness

Do you believe you have encountered a burning-bush moment with God? What has the Lord used as your burning bush? Are you ready to proclaim His name to others?

_____

_____

_____

_____

_____

_____

_____

_____

_____

How can hope and confidence in Jesus Christ affect your proclaiming to others?

_____

_____

_____

_____

_____

_____

_____

_____

_____

_____

_____

_____

_____

Chapter 14

Proclaim God's Blessings and Return

Proclaim God's Blessings for the Faithful

> For the eyes of the Lord are on the righteous, and
> His ears are open to their prayers; but the face of the
> Lord is against those who do evil.—1 Peter 3:12

First Peter 3:12 tells us to proclaim the fact that God hears the prayers and pleas of His people. If we are living a life modeled after Jesus Christ's example, then we are seeking that righteousness of which Peter is speaking. We saw in the last chapter and throughout this book how God will be with us. God will bless us and be faithful to our requests when given to Him from a pure heart and for His glory. God will have His hand upon us, shelter us, and be receptive to our needs and prayers. Proclaim this intimacy to others. Encourage and lift up others during their times of doubt and questioning. Assure them that God's Spirit is present with them and will give them peace, if sought.

Noah was obedient to God and followed the calling God had given him. As a result, God tells Noah:

"And as for Me, behold, I establish My covenant with you and with your descendants after you" (Genesis 9:9).

After Israel has repented for their transgressions, God says He will establish a new covenant with them.

"But this is the covenant that I will make with the house of Israel after those days, says the Lord: I will put My law in their minds, and write it on their hearts; and I will be their God, and they shall be My people" (Jeremiah 31:33).

In these two verses, God tells us of covenants He will make to His people. Jeremiah points to the new covenant through Jesus Christ and repentance for past sins. Genesis tells us of God's establishing a covenant with us after obedience. We have made the repentance for our past sins through our belief and confession in Jesus Christ—God's new covenant. We have surrendered, believed, and lived as God has instructed. Throughout this transformation, God has placed His Law in our minds and written it upon our hearts. We are partakers of this covenant with God. We are the people of the almighty God—chosen, forgiven, freed, and anointed to proclaim this salvation. God will not turn His back on His people. God will not break His covenant. God is faithful to His people. Proclaim this faithfulness!

First Peter 3:12 also tells us we are to proclaim God's anger toward those who turn away from Him. This is somewhat of a tricky area. A lot of human error can occur when pointing out someone's faults, but we can do this with confidence and love. It is possible to convict fellow brothers' and sisters' hearts without condemning their souls. We can share our testimonies to all those who will listen. If we see a brother struggling, we can relate to him through conversation how we struggled as well and what we found to deliver us. When there are circumstances that cause us to distance ourselves from others, we often are asked to explain ourselves. We are given an opportunity to share our testimonies and faith with them. The choice is theirs on whether or not they hear the testimonies. We are obedient and have done our part when we give them.

During these opportunities, be sure to stress the life of bondage you knew, as compared to the sense of freedom you now enjoy. As a proclaimer for Christ, you must act upon these opportunities. Do not be ashamed of the gospel. If you are, your Lord will also be ashamed of you. Pray for true ability through the Holy Spirit to let you see the hearts of those still suffering and struggling. As Christians, we seek further souls to share the kingdom of heaven with our Lord. If we only proclaim to those who are saved, how do we accomplish helping others to know Jesus Christ? Second Timothy 3:12 will come into play again when proclaiming to the lost.

There's no doubt we will suffer persecutions during these times, but there also will be times when some will hear our testimony and as a result, they will become open and conscious toward making a decision of giving their lives to Jesus Christ. This decision may be an immediate one we get to witness and in which we rejoice, or it may be one that will come in the future for that individual. No matter what the case may be, remember God has a covenant with you that He will not break.

Proclaim this truth to yourself as well. You have the Father's attention! The Lord is waiting to hear your requests that will further His kingdom. You are the kingdom, a vessel that contains the goodness and righteousness of God. The Spirit of God dwells in you, wishing not only to govern your inner kingdom granted to you by the Lord, but to extend the kingdom into the lives of those around you. You have the audience of God, which has a will to reach and reconcile the world to Him through you. Align your will with the will of God.

Many times in my worldly life, I begged God to align His will with my will. I was unwilling to align my will with His. Therefore, God did not give many of my requests and desires (which stemmed from selfishness and fear) His blessing and attention. How could of He have given this? I was asking God to compromise His holiness and purpose for me and those around me. The face of the Lord is against those who do evil. I was one of those evildoers throughout my life, with unawareness of the fact I was. But now I have been focusing on aligning my will with the will of the Father. Much different results come to pass once we seek God's direction and path. God's heart is reflected by His children's hearts here on earth. God will be attentive and watchful of our needs, requests, and successes. We are fulfilling His purpose through our lives. How could God deny His children from furthering His kingdom? He could not! Therefore, proclaim with humility but boldness and confidence that the Lord's hand is upon you. He will fight your battles. God does, will, and shall bless His faithful followers.

Proclaim the Return of the King

> Therefore, since all these things will be dissolved, what manner *of persons* ought you to be in holy conduct and godliness, looking for and hastening the coming of the day of God, because of which the heavens will be dissolved, being on fire, and the elements will melt with fervent heat? Nevertheless we, according to His promise, look for new heaven and a new earth in which righteousness dwells.—2 Peter 3:11–13

In 2 Peter 3:12, we are led to proclaim that all we know on earth will be dissolved and Jesus Christ, King of Kings, will return. Peter tells us in this chapter that the day of the Lord will indeed come and will come as a thief in the night. The world as we know it will no longer exist. All will be made new. Are we to stand on the corners of our cities with signs that read "The end is near—repent"? My heart is not leading me that way. I believe we are to proclaim God's beautiful promise of eternity with Him. There will be new heavens and a new earth where righteousness dwells. If righteousness dwells upon the coming heavens and earth, who will dwell there? Obviously, the righteous will be the inhabitants, not those who think they are righteous.

Proclaim Christ's return when He will call His righteous home with Him. Second Peter 3:11–13 coincides with 1 Peter perfectly on the topic of "Proclaim." Both verses tell us to remain faithful to God and proclaim His promises to His people. We also see in both verses the need to proclaim to those not living as God has taught and the longing God has for them to join Him.

"The Lord is not slack concerning His promise, as some count slackness, but is longsuffering toward us, not willing that any should perish but that all should come to repentance" (2 Peter 3:9).

We should reflect the same attitude in our proclaiming as God has. The more we witness of Jesus Christ, the more we share our stories of transformation and the more hope we spread to those yet to know of God's mercy and love. Also, we need to hold fellow Christians accountable as well as ourselves. Let's remind each other that God is in control. Stand shoulder-to-shoulder with one another and further strengthen each other in Christ.

Another theme that is very popular and still gaining steam in the world today are the questions, "How can a loving God allow all the evil in the world and let innocent people get hurt? How can God allow innocent children to be assaulted?" These questions are exactly why we need to put First and Second Peter 3:12 into action through our faith and proclaiming. God will not allow all the wickedness to take place. God is a loving God and will bring an end to this madness run amok by the wicked world in which we live. I believe it is only due to God's great love for us that He is holding off His return. God is allowing us to choose repentance through His Son and have salvation. The book of Revelation clearly states God's disapproval of the wicked actions of mankind. Jesus Christ will return and bring an end to all this chaos and tragedy. Jesus will bring an end to all the misery that much of the world is blaming on God's nonexistence and lack of love. This day will come! If we are not seeking righteousness through Jesus Christ, we will not be inhabitants of the new world our loving God will provide us.

We have been given rebirth. Many in the world are still in bondage and sin. We must stay focused on God's calling and Jesus's teachings to remain in the truth. We are to follow God's Word and agenda.

Many people in the world spread false doctrine and false hope and promote sinful lifestyles for their own gain. God will honor His righteous people. Proclaim that honor and faith you have in God. Witness and guide those in need of the truth. Take upon yourself this responsibility God has given you. The responsibility will not be one of burden but one of joy and peace. Do not try to hold out and keep from being contaminated in the world. I am not saying to place yourself in a position that could harm you or others, but don't be timid in the position of proclaiming your faith. Yes, the Lord has given you forgiveness and eternity. But he also instructs us to return that great treasure into the world that it may multiply and be fruitful. Jesus Christ Himself gave us instruction on how to proclaim.

"Go into all the world and preach the gospel to every creature. He who believes and is baptized will be saved; he who does not believe will be condemned" (Mark 15:15–16).

We are confident of our future and eternity. We know exactly where we are going. It is tempting at times to long for that eternity with Christ in heaven and leave the cares of this world behind. Even in our most peaceful moments, remnants of the world still remain, concerns and obligations that can linger in our thoughts. We can become weary and tired, and at times it may seem like nothing around us is changing. Understandably, we long for the future and our Promised Land in heaven with the Lord. How could we not? However, we are guaranteed it will come. For the remainder of our days here on earth, we are to be the words of faith and hope for others to see.

"For to me, to live is Christ, and to die is gain. But if I live on in the flesh, this will mean fruit from my labor; yet what I shall choose I cannot tell. For I am hard-pressed between the two, having a desire to depart and be with Christ, which is far better. Nevertheless to remain in the flesh is more needful for you" (Philippians 1:21–24).

Be the righteous of Jesus Christ and faithful men of God. Carry the message of hope for the world to see. Proclaim this great love that God has for all His children. The world as we know it will indeed come to an end. But let us be diligent and obedient disciples of Jesus Christ, and through His Word and Spirit, call all we can to join us in the world without end that God will establish in place of this one.

Proclaim God's Blessings for the Faithful

In what areas can you proclaim God's faithfulness in your life? How can your proclaiming be used by God to influence others?

_____

_____

_____

_____

_____

_____

_____

_____

_____

Proclaim the Return of the King

Rather than fear and a doomsday speech, how can we reach people for Christ to encourage them to be prepared for the new heavens and earth that will be established?

_____

_____

_____

_____

_____

_____

_____

_____

_____

Chapter 15

Proclaim the Promises of Jesus Christ!

He who overcomes, I will make him a pillar in the temple of
My God, and he shall go out no more. I will write on him the
name of My God and the name of the city of My God, the New
Jerusalem, which comes down out of heaven from My God.
And I will write on him My new name.—Revelation 3:12

The final verse in 3:12 Transformation is quite a promise from our
Lord, Jesus Christ. Jesus has a lot of plans for our future, not only
in this lifetime but the one to come as well. This chapter will focus
on proclaiming this promise to others, but first and foremost, I want
you to personally proclaim this promise to yourself.

This verse represents Jesus's speaking to the apostle John, the writer
of the book of Revelation. Jesus is addressing the seven churches that
have been established up to that point. Jesus is telling those in the
church to persevere, have faith, and stand true in His teachings. He
then speaks what we read in Revelation 3:12. He speaks to those
who overcome the lies and tribulations of this world and those
who will repent for their sinful lives and overcome the world they
have known by their faith in Jesus Christ. Jesus tells how He will
claim those overcomers—He will write His name upon them. He
will write on them the name of His God and the name of the city

of His God—the New Jerusalem. Jesus takes 100 percent ownership of those who overcome. He will reward them with paradise, peace, joy, and His presence forever.

We are those overcomers. We are the ones Jesus Christ is claiming. All the promises that are written are for you and me to share together with Christ, our Lord. Our overcoming is made simple when we surrender to Jesus Christ and let Him bear our burdens that once overcame us. We truly need to overcome ourselves and this world. It can be done through the blood of Jesus Christ but not on our own. Jesus is pleading with us to overcome our fears, worries, selfishness, pain, and struggles and give them to Him with faith. God loves us so much more than words can say. Why else would He have created us, given us chance after chance, sacrificed His Son for us, and then given one encouragement after another as spiritual guidance throughout the Scriptures? God tells us we have overcome.

"For whatever is born of God overcomes the world. And this is the victory that has overcome the world—our faith" (1 John 5:4).

There is the faith key again. Our faith—our belief—is what enables our victory in Christ and over this world. Through our faith, we overcome. Proclaim your faith for all to know. Proclaim your faith for the world to know. Shout with your spirit, "I am an overcomer in Christ!" Proclaim this to yourself and believe it. God cannot lie. God says the overcomers will be the victors, and the wicked will not defeat us. Do not hate the wicked and the lifestyle they lead, which at times seems like they will never be held accountable for it. God tells us:

"These will make war with the Lamb, and the Lamb will overcome them, for He is Lord of lords and King of Kings; and those who are with Him are called, chosen, and faithful" (Revelation 17:14).

Proclaim your future victory with Christ to yourself and to all those who hear you. Witness to others in faith and hope that they can join the winning side of Jesus Christ. What does it mean to you that you have overcome and will go out no more? To me, it makes all the difference for my surrender, belief, and life I will live. When I contemplate the reality that Jesus Christ Himself is telling me, "He shall go out no more" (Revelation 3:12), it takes it to a spiritual level for which words seem inadequate. The feelings of worthlessness will not return. The doubt of eternity and what it involves is gone. The urgency of claiming victory in the human race is no longer important. My marriage will not be threatened again by my selfish actions. My family will come to know Jesus Christ and live their lives for Him when their time with God becomes known. I will go out no more. I will not turn my back on my God. I am told I will be made a pillar in the temple of God.

A pillar is a structure of strength that supports and bears the weight of another structure. The structure we are being made to support is the temple of God, not a simple building by this world's standard. As soon as we surrender and give our lives to Jesus, the pillars we are to become begins a molding process through the blood of Christ. This pillar will be made from materials of faith and obedience. It will be cast and cured to stand the test of time for the eternal kingdom of God. On earth, our pillars will support the church of Jesus Christ, which will extend into heaven for God's Spirit to rest upon and govern from. As pillars for Christ. we are establishing the kingdom of God here upon the earth.

What does the word "overcome" say to you? What does "Go out no more" mean to you? What does being made a pillar mean to you? It needs to mean everything, and most of all, you need to believe!

"He who overcomes shall inherit all things, and I will be His God and he shall be My son" (Revelation 21:7).

God wants to give you all things. It makes all the little things we chased in life seem pretty futile, doesn't it? We are sons and daughters of God. Our Father wants to give us inheritance to share with Jesus Christ. Proclaim this beautiful promise. Where do you turn from here if you do not accept? Once you know the peace and presence of God, can you turn away? Where would you go? What would you do? Who will fight your battles—the ones you cannot win? Who will sacrifice his or her life for you? We all like to be the winner; nobody wishes to be on the losing team. If you are reading this book and do not know Jesus Christ as your personal Lord and Savior, ask Him to become that now. You do not want to risk another day, another year, or another ten years. Jesus Christ will come as a thief in the night upon His return. Please don't be caught on the losing team. Give your life to Jesus. Be an overcomer and win! For those of you who have given your lives to Christ, I challenge you to look at the life you are leading for Him. Are you doing everything you can for the spread of the kingdom of God? Have we become so comfortable with our own salvation that the salvation of our brothers and sisters is no longer a priority? Are we proclaiming Jesus Christ and the gift He has given us? Have we become lukewarm in our walk with Christ?

We can all do more, give more, and believe more. It is our responsibility to unite all the denominations of Christianity as one unified church in the name of Jesus Christ, our Lord. As pillars of the temple of God, we must perform the following steps:

1. Surrender our pride and unproductive rivalries among each other.
2. Believe we are all fellow brothers and sisters in Christ, called as a whole for His glory.
3. Live a life that exemplifies to others the need to join in living for Christ and live by God's Word, not by our compromises.

4. Proclaim the peace and beauty to which a life in Christ will lead by our testimonies.

Proclaim the Promises of Jesus Christ!

What has Jesus Christ overcome for you?

_____

_____

_____

_____

_____

_____

_____

_____

_____

_____

Can you picture yourself as a pillar for the Lord?

_____

_____

_____

_____

_____

_____

_____

_____

_____

_____

_____

In your own words, share the promise God has made to you as your belief and faith whisper His voice within your heart.

_____

_____

_____

_____

_____

_____

_____

_____

_____

_____

_____

_____

_____

Closing Thoughts and Prayers

I want to encourage all of you. It makes no difference if you are a new Christian or a lifelong follower of Christ. We all play a role in God's direction for this earth. I believe God is calling His people to return to Him and make ready for the future events that will take place. God is giving mercy and blessings to those willing and seeking to receive them. The divisional lines are being clearly drawn in the world. You either live for God, or you are chasing evil through the short-term gains of living for the world. I believe God's Holy Spirit is descending upon the earth at this time in history so those who will be saved will recognize and be given strength through faith. I also believe this is for the sole purpose of saving as many souls as possible for God's will and the great love He has for all. God's Holy Spirit will ripple across this earth for all to know. For those who believe, it will be a rushing tidal wave of truth that convicts their souls.

Father, please let Your people come to You completely with open and humble hearts. Let us know Your great wisdom, peace, mercies, and love. Lord, through Your Son, Jesus Christ, may we follow the guidance You have given us. May our souls be set ablaze for Your glory and magnification, Lord. Search our hearts and our minds and remove anything that offends You, Father. Give us the strength needed to trust in Your holiness and peace of mind in knowing You are our provider. Father, rise up your church through Your Holy Spirit to become what Jesus Christ, our Lord, sacrificed Himself for it to be, according to Your infinite wisdom. And Father, give us courage to sacrifice our fears, so others may know You as well. In the name of Your Son, Jesus Christ, and through the power of Your Holy Spirit, we ask this of You, Father. Amen.

When I was first developing 3:12 Transformation, I felt the desire to capture what I believed it truly expressed, so that anyone could understand the program fairly easily and quickly. As a result, God revealed to me a poem that contains fifteen verses from the program. I have added it to the ending of this book with the hope it will read as God's message to you individually, as it did to me. May you desire to know God more each day!

3:12 Transformation Poem

My child,
I will be with you; do not be afraid.
I will show others the commitment we've made (Exodus 3:12),

For my child, I dearly love you; I'll correct your evil ways.
And you will sense My Spirit, each and every day (Proverbs 3:12;
Ezekiel 3:12).

I will remove your foolish pride and the doubts of your soul
And fill it with humility till it overflows (Zephaniah 3:12).

My child, believe these words I am telling you
And enter into My kingdom when judgment day comes due (John
3:12).

I will give you hope and confidence and tell you how to speak.
You will call upon My Son with boldness in your speech (2
Corinthians 3:12; Ephesians 3:12).

Now, child, strive to be perfect, though you'll never get there,
For My Son, He is perfect, and your sin He did bear (Philippians
3:12).

Now I will fill your heart with kindness and with love
And always give the same mercies you've been given from above
(Colossians 3:12).

I will show you new ways to love each other more;
The love that comes back to you, far greater than before (1 Thessalonians 3:12).

My child, as we take this journey, beware what lies in store;
This world will try to attack you and lead you to death once more (2 Timothy 3:12).

But stand fast in My love; don't trust their wicked ways,
For if the fruit I've given starts to spoil, all could rot away (Hebrew 3:12; James 3:12).

My Spirit will watch over you; I'll guide you along the way,
But to those who live for evil, I'll not hear a word they say (1 Peter 3:12).

My child, when this world has ended, and evil has been cast down,
You'll be among My precious overcomers, wearing My victor's crown (Revelation 3:12).

—With guidance and love from your Creator

Printed in the United States
By Bookmasters